INSPIRING HOPE

One Story at a Time

*All the best in
what you do, Judy!*

Gary

Compiled by Gary Doi

Opinions expressed by one author do not necessarily reflect the perspectives of the other authors.

Printed in U.S.A. in 2013.

This book can be purchased at www.amazon.com, www.amazon.co.uk, and www.amazon.ca

For inquiries contact editor@ahopefulsign.com.

ISBN-13: 978-1492847441
ISBN-10: 1492847445

TO ALL THOSE WHO INSPIRE HOPE

ALL NET PROCEEDS FROM BOOK SALES will be donated to the Asturias Academy Library in Xela, Guatemala—a private, non-profit Pre K-12 school dedicated to helping the most vulnerable students in the community. For more information, visit the school's website (asturiasacademy.org).

Table of Contents

INTRODUCTION   1

LEARNING TO LIVE   5
PART 1: This Moment   7
The Night Blooming Cereus in our Life   ZEE GORMAN
Dimes From Dad   JOHN MCLAUGHLIN
Breathing in Island Park   CAROLYN SOLARES
The Secret of My Happiness   ZEE GORMAN
Why I Love Running in the Rain   JOHN MCLAUGHLIN
Kids Do Say the Darndest Things   GARY DOI
Of Geese and Men   RICK COGBILL
A River Runs Through Me   BRUCE MASTERMAN
A Magical Moment   GARY DOI

PART 2: The Traveller Sees   29
A Lifetime of Adventure: The Vogel Family   NANCY SATHRE-VOGEL
Following in the Steps of Emperors   FRANCISCO LITTLE
Will I Have to Wear a Burqa?   CATHERINE SUNDHER
Ignorance is Bliss   FRANCISCO LITTLE
A Walk on the Wild Side   VALLI-L. FRASER-CELIN
ALMS on Beggar's Road   FRANCISCO LITTLE
30 Days of Ramadan   CATHERINE SUNDHER
The Way to Santiago   CHERINA HADLEY
Just a Walk in the Park   FRANCISCO LITTLE
Stories of My Generation   GUY TAL

PART 3: The Love of Family   56
Saying Yes to Whatever the Future Holds   BECKY ROBINSON

I'm Molly McClelland, Jeffrey's Mom — MOLLY MCCLELLAND

How Mama Got Her Happy Groove Back — TARA RUMMELL BERSON

The Bar Mitzvah Boy — AIMEE LEDEWITZ WEINSTEIN

Regret is Dead Weight — KAREN VELEZ

No Longer "New" Mom — MOLLY MCCLELLAND

Heading Out - Starting Them Young — BRUCE MASTERMAN

You Gotta Have Hope — AIMEE LEDEWITZ WEINSTEIN

Bibliophiles and Bookworms — BECKY ROBINSON

Lessons From My Son — KAREN VELEZ

The Secret to a Happy Marriage — JOHN MCLAUGHLIN

Reinventing Mama — AIMEE LEDEWITZ WEINSTEIN

My Grandfather's Determination — DEBORAH FIKE

At Age 102, Margaret Dunning Drives to College — DEBRA EVE

Eulogy for My Grandfather — JODI AMAN

Is Your Door Open? — CATHRYN WELLNER

PART 4: Obstacles to Overcome 98

Clearing Out the Weeds (In the Garden of Our Life) — SHARON REED

Lessons Learned From Being Bullied — COLLEEN CANNEY

Watch Out for that Rough Section Ahead — LAURA BEST

The Beat of a Different Drum — CAROLYN SOLARES

Living with Depression — DEBORAH SERANI

Sometimes, You Just Have to Say No — CATHRYN WELLNER

It's Hard to Lose Something You Love — CARRIE ELLEN BRUMMER

How to Find Perspective in a Hard Moment — BECKY ROBINSON

LIVING TO LEARN 117

Follow Your Passion — NINA MUNTEANU

5 Simple Steps to Achieve Your Goals — KAARINA DILLABOUGH

What Does Work-Life Balance Mean Anyway? — COLLEEN CANNEY

Lessons Learned from the Food Service Industry — LINDA POURMASSINA

Bucket List — CARRIE ELLEN BRUMMER

Why We Need to Write   NINA MUNTEANU

Creating Hopeful Futures for Youth   MARILYN PRICE-MITCHELL

Choice not Chance   KAARINA DILLABOUGH

Making Life and Work a Work of Art   LINDA NAIMAN

What Will You Do in Retirement?   ANN HARRISON

What Are You Packing on Life's Journey?   KAARINA DILLABOUGH

Four Occasions When It's Best to Keep Quiet   GWYN TEATRO

Are You Living in the Middle of the Hunger Games?   IAN LAWTON

Millions Saw the Apple Fall, but Newton Asked Why   CONNIE DENESIUK

Seven Habits of Highly Creative People   LINDA NAIMAN

How to Accept Rejection   NINA MUNTEANU

Keeping an Open Mind   ZEE GORMAN

10 Steps to Learning How to Live Joyfully   GAIL BRENNER

Want to Make a Change in Your Life?   ANN HARRISON

MAKING A DIFFERENCE   **169**

Bertha Benz's Wild Ride   DEBRA EVE

Chief Clarence Louie: Nation Builder   CONNIE DENESIUK

Have You Had Your Hug Today?   MELINDA SCHMITT

Meet George the Cabbie   SHARON REED

The Teacher Who Handed Us a Whole New World   HEATHER ONDERICK

Why Did I Become an Educator?   CARRIE ELLEN BRUMMER

Me to We: Student Leadership in Action   PAIGE SKOFTEBY

Students "Make Art for Change"   JENNIFER CACACI

Change the World in 3 Minutes   GARY DOI

Hope Heals at Ted E. Bear Hollow   NANCY HEMESATH

Commemorating the 3/11 Disaster   AIMEE LEDEWITZ WEINSTEIN

LWB in Guatemala   SAMHITA GUPTA

The Price of Hope   ZEE GORMAN

Introduction

"There is hope in dreams, imagination, and in the courage of those who wish to make those dreams a reality." - Jonas Salk

By GARY DOI (Penticton, British Columbia) September 2013

This all began as an experiment of sorts.

Not a scientific one, but a test nonetheless to determine if there was a common bond, linkage or interest amongst the millions of bloggers out there for what I was trying to sell. (After all, most blog sites are trying to sell something. Right?)

I was trying to sell an idea. I was trying to tap into the finer spirit of hope and the generosity and talents of bloggers everywhere.

My big ask?

The age-old question: What gives you hope?

More specifically, is there a real-life story you have written or were prepared to write about a hopeful experience? It could be a personal story reflecting life's highs and lows, an anecdote of an important work-related or life lesson or an inspirational narrative of a difference-maker.

We created the magazine blog, *A Hopeful Sign*, as the public forum, the platform for sharing these stories on the internet. In May, 2011 we launched the all-volunteer site with a mere handful of submissions. However, in the two years between then and June 2013, when the blog concluded, we posted well over 500 stories! We were fortunate indeed to have so many writers take up the challenge. Artists, authors, photographers, students, educators, doctors, professors, lawyers, coaches, media specialists, managers and parents willingly shared their stories and viewpoints with us. Along the way, we featured inspirational videos, a Facebook fan page and a stunning photo gallery.

This charity book project is an off-shoot of that collaboration—in content, in design and in spirit. Zee Gorman (IT manager, San Francisco) was the first to suggest and rally others to the idea of publishing a book featuring the "best of the best" from *A Hopeful Sign*. Having successfully self-published her own books, she volunteered to manage the online publishing process. Zee was a tremendous resource and I am truly thankful for her leadership. Carrie Brummer (teacher/artist, Dubai) also lent considerable time and talent in creating the wonderful "tree of life" artwork for the book cover and section dividers. Somehow she managed to find the time despite a jam-packed summer schedule which included getting married, going on a honeymoon and finding a new home! Thank you, Carrie, for all that you brought to this project. I am also grateful to our many writers who stepped up to help with proofreading and edits and responding to my questions. Questions such as: Should spelling be standardized or reflect the writer's country of origin? (We decided to go with the latter.) Does the cover design have universal appeal and a hopeful nature? (The first design concept was soundly rejected!) How can we reach the broadest possible market? (This last question was particularly important as all net proceeds will be donated to provide resource support for the Asturias Academy Library in Xela, Guatemala, one of the hopeful stories in this book.)

Inspiring Hope: One Story at a Time features seventy-five stories by forty-two writers, organized into three interrelated sections—Learning to Live; Living to Learn; and Making a Difference. The writers come from various age groups, diverse backgrounds and different parts of the world. For example, a California mother (and part-time lawyer) shares her heartfelt story about raising an autistic child and how that experience brought fulfillment, love and gratitude. A New Brunswick maritimer explains why his secret to a happy marriage is a pair of rocking chairs and two good quilts. A teacher in Dubai describes how her bucket-list adventures opened up fascinating opportunities to learn and discover. A retirement coach from the United Kingdom explores a common question facing retirees: What will I do with the rest of my life? A sixteen-year-old student in Tokyo rallies people to provide aid to a small fishing village affected by the Tohoku Earthquake disaster. And, a South African-born artist describes a disconcerting experience walking along Beggar's Road in India as the impoverished hopefuls line a dirt road for three kilometres — waiting for the generosity of strangers.

The stories are as varied and far-reaching as life itself. They are startlingly honest. They stir the imagination, summon your courage and invite reflection. They speak to your inner voice.

They inspire hope.

Now that's something we can all use more of.

Gary Doi served as Superintendent of Schools for eighteen years in three school districts in British Columbia. Previous to that, he was a teacher, school administrator and university lecturer. He created the magazine blog, "A Hopeful Sign" (ahopeful-sign.com), as he believes there is no greater force for creating change than hope.

Learning to Live

"There is no passion to be found playing small, in settling for a life that is less than the one you are capable of living." - Nelson Mandela

PART 1: THIS MOMENT

"Be happy for this moment. This moment is your life."

- Omar Khayyam

The Night Blooming Cereus in Our Life

By ZEE GORMAN (San Francisco, California) 21 October 2011

Night Blooming Cereus (a.k.a. Epiphyllum strictum) is a type of flower that only blooms for a short period of time and yet they are fiercely beautiful and pleasantly fragrant. My mother used to have one on her front porch. One summer night we sat around a blossoming bud and watched it go from shyly opening to fully blossoming, and then to tiredly closed-up, within hours. I have always been fascinated by them.

There are people in our life that are like a Night Blooming Cereus. They brush shoulders with us for only a short period of time but leave long-lasting impressions on us. I bet if you think hard, you'll be able to name one or two in your life. Though even if you think hard, you may not be able to name exactly what they did to have claimed a spot in your heart.

Annette is one of the Night Blooming Cereus in my life.

I met her in my first graduate class in the United States. Being new to the country and not knowing the ins and outs of my environment, I tried to keep to myself. Sitting down in my chair with my empty backpack (I just arrived the day before), I sensed a pair of eyes on me behind my right shoulder. I turned slightly and was met by a bright smile of a woman with an oval face, large hazel eyes, and long golden hair.

"What is your name?" she asked.

I was either too shy or too overwhelmed by my surroundings

to answer her in time. So she said again, "My name is Annette. What is yours?"

"Oh. Zi-Hong."

"Zi-Hong," she repeated. "It's a beautiful name!"

I smiled politely as an answer. I was still not used to responding to compliments the American way. In China, the custom is to humbly deny it by saying, "Na, not at all."

"How do you say it in your native language?" Annette continued to show great interest in my name, which I never thought to be beautiful.

"Tze-Hong," I said it in Mandarin. Her big eyes stared at my lips and mimicked their movements studiously. She made a couple attempts and asked if she sounded right. Then she laughed in a bright voice at her awkward pronunciation. "That's fascinating!" she said.

"It's very nice to meet you, Zi-Hong. I see you don't have a textbook yet. You can share mine. Come sit closer to me. Do you know where to get your textbooks? I can take you to the bookstore

I never saw her again. Deep down in my heart, I know that I've enjoyed the gift she brought me all these years.

after class if you want. . . ."

I just nodded and said "thank you" after every other sentence.

"Do I speak too fast for you? Just tell me to slow down. If you have trouble following the professor, I'll share my notes with you." She went on until the professor started the class. Then she stuck her tongue out, winked, and leaned back to pay attention to the lecture.

I was so overwhelmed by her helpfulness that after the class, I escaped out of her sight. I told my Chinese friends about her and they asked me if she was a Native American, a Hispanic, or a Caucasian. I said I couldn't tell. The next day I pointed her out to my friends, and they laughed. "She's 100% white. You can't even tell that?"

Nope. The truth is everybody looked the same to me. I took note of her appearance. She seemed to love to wear a long skirt, knee-high leather boots, and colorful gem stone jewelry. They looked befitting to her tall slender figure. She reminded me of the Gypsies.

I was a bit embarrassed by my disappearance the first day so I gathered the courage to walk up to her and greet her. She was so happy to see me that she hugged me. Then she asked how I did in my first day and if I found everything alright. Whatever she was doing, she finally put me at ease.

I came to the realization that I could do no wrong with her.

At the end of my first week, she invited me to her house for the weekend. She lived in a small wooden cottage with two bedrooms upstairs and a kitchen/living room downstairs. Log benches, Southwestern style rugs, and dream catchers gave the place a rustic feel. She had a 10-year-old son by the name of Gabriel. I learned that she had lived on an Indian reservation for many years. Her husband had died of cancer when Gabriel was born and she was now dating an American Indian man. He owned a garage on the reservation and only came up here to see her occasionally. And I told her briefly of my childhood and my upbringing in China.

She said thoughtfully after my story. "I think all that hardship brought you here. It is meant to be."

I slept in her living room that night.

The next day I woke up to bright crystals blinking in the sun light and the gentle sound of a wind chime singing on the porch. I had never felt so peaceful in my life. All my worries, stress, and uncertainty about a new life in a new country dissolved.

I felt only beauty around me.

Later that semester, Annette quit school and went back to the reservation to be married to her lover. I never saw her again. Deep down in my heart, I know that I've enjoyed the gift she brought me all these years.

Zee Gorman (zeegorman.blogspot.ca), *born in Southern China during the Cultural Revolution (both her parents were exiled to the countryside for being "intellectuals"), was raised within layers of political and cultural confines. Yet her love for literature gave wings to a life that is very different from what it is destined to be. She has written short stories, poems, and essays, and is mildly published in China. Her quest for a better life eventually led to her migration to the United States where she completed two Master's Degrees. Today, Zee Gorman lives in Northern California with her husband and her daughter. By night she is a writer, an artist, a crafter... whatever she imagines herself to be and by day she has a career in IT management.*

Dimes From Dad

By JOHN MCLAUGHLIN (Bathurst, New Brunswick) 18 July 2011

My father started me on a coin collection. It's an interesting collection, you might think, because it's comprised exclusively of dimes. And as of today, I have sixty-eight of them.

Dad never actually handed me these coins. It was only after he passed away, two years ago, that dimes started to appear. At first it seemed an odd occurrence, a dime here or there, unexpectedly.

Never pennies. Never nickels. Just dimes.

Everyone in my family's been finding them, and they seem to come when we need them most: a pat of reassurance, a shot of courage, a wink from Heaven. We're all convinced these are dimes from Dad.

Here's a typical discovery: I'd been anxious about a difficult situation at work, and when it finally came time to make the tough phone call, I said to myself "Dad, if I could ever use a dime, it's now." I walked a few meters, and nestled in shrubs was a shiny dime, Bluenose up. I made the call, and everything went well.

Another: my brother was dealing with a high pressure situation at work. "What am I supposed to do?" he asked himself. In seconds, his eye shot to a dime, a calming dime, where none should have been. He got the job done.

Every dime in my little container tells a similar story. Each brought a message from Dad, usually something like "You're doing just fine, son," or "You know very well how to handle this!"

We all cherish our dimes, because they give us hope. Every new discovery brings a blissful rush, a hug between souls. They tell us to live confidently, joyously, purposefully. And so, as if children once again, we happily accept our pocket change from Dad, a regular allowance paid with love in Heaven's currency.

INSPIRING HOPE — ONE STORY AT A TIME

John McLaughlin is Deputy Minister at the New Brunswick Department of Education & Early Childhood Development. As a former teacher and super-intendent of schools, he believes the highest goal of education should be to nurture in students a sense of goodness, so they graduate from high school equipped not just with strong academic skills, but also a desire to contribute positively to the world, and to care for its people. John and his wife, Cathy, have four grown daughters, and they live in Bathurst on New Brunswick's beautiful northeastern coast.

Breathing in Island Park

By CAROLYN SOLARES (Minneapolis, Minnesota) 28 June 2011

A beautiful city park sits near downtown Fargo, North Dakota, a city not especially known for its natural beauty. I returned to Fargo as an adult—and ended up staying for five years. While living there, I spent many hours walking around the perimeter of this small park, which covers one city block and is home to hundreds of care-fully planted trees and flowers, making it look like an urban forest.

I have childhood memories of taking swimming and tennis lessons there, attending festivals and picnics there, and cutting through the park on the way to the YMCA, which shares its northeast corner. As an adult, however, I largely appreciated the park from the outside looking in, staying on the pavement surrounding it. But one day last summer, I followed inspiration into the park. Standing in the middle of the trees and grass, I saw something I had never noticed before. People come here alone; they come here to be alone. And I marveled that a place that attracts so many solo visitors would be so appropriately named... Island Park.

I have always thought of this pretty, tree-covered park as a happy place. Yet I have come to recognize it as well as a lonely, melancholy place—a welcoming space inviting its visitors to leave their loneliness and their melancholia, if only for a moment, in the park.

I went there a lot to think and to breathe. And I went there to walk, not my usual rapid power-walking, but calm, thoughtful steps. I brought my hopes, my worries, and my sorrows. But the park never seemed to mind. In return for these meager offerings, it always made a miraculous and unequal exchange, generously depositing a piece of itself in me.

On the north edge of the park stands a bronze and granite statue called Angel of Hope, a memorial to families who have lost children. For whatever reason, this corner became my favorite place in the park. I'd sit there quietly on one of the iron benches in front of the statue, looking at the bricks in the pavements with names of children who had died, all strangers to me. I felt some-

 I have always thought of this pretty, tree-covered park as a happy place. Yet I have come to recognize it as well as a lonely, melancholy place ...

thing comforting and sweet, even sacred, about this spot. I stopped there to think, to not think, and sometimes to just listen. And I loved the families who, in creating this little oasis of hope, made it safe for all visitors to release our own heartache and sorrow. I came to think of this angel as my angel, and I always felt better after visiting her.

On one of my last walks through the park, I watched two teenage boys walking on the grass, and assumed they were using the park as a shortcut. Then they surprised me and sat on one of the benches in front of my angel. But I shouldn't have been surprised. They recognized the bittersweet magic of that special spot. I smiled knowing that my angel was now also their angel — and that none of us are ever really alone.

Last November, I moved to a city with no shortage of natural beauty. Yet while recently walking around a pretty lake in a suburban park, I found myself missing the small tree-covered park, my solo companions, and our angel of hope. As I wound my way around the narrow lake feeling optimism, joy, and peace, I knew that the park I loved — that had given me so much — was still with me. And I thanked my angel and the healing power of that island park.

Carolyn Solares is a writer, artist, business strategist—and recovering MBA. She lives in Minneapolis, where she writes about the journey of living a happy life. Visit her online at www.carolynsolares.com.

The Secret of My Happiness

By ZEE GORMAN (San Francisco, California) 23 July 2011

On the day I turned 40, I felt unprecedentedly depressed. This is it, I thought to myself. There's no question whatsoever now that I belong to the "no longer young" category.

I have seen women like me in department stores, grocery stores or wherever they run their errands. They look boring and uninteresting, their faces tired and their bodies out of shape. They are unattractive. And now I am one of them. None of my concerns about my appearance matter anymore: My waist size, my glasses, the ten extra pounds I put on after I gave birth to my daughter, or my thinning hair that is getting harder to style. . . . None of those things matter anymore. Why bother? No matter what I do, I won't look young ever again!

I asked my husband to take a picture of me. To be as realistic as possible, I didn't style my hair or put on any make-up. I didn't even put on a smile. He did as I said. The picture came out and confirmed everything I thought of myself—old, frumpy, unsexy. I captioned it: Mom turns 40.

Indeed, I am a mom. My life as "me" is over. It is now my daughter's turn.

I looked at myself again in the mirror and sighed: I might as well get used to it. It would only get worse from this point on.

The next day I phoned up Jeff — who is gay and has been my best friend since graduate school. He gave me his belated birthday wishes and I told him about my state of mind. He paused and then reminded me that I have a very good life; I have a loving husband, a beautiful daughter, and a great career. It is something I couldn't imagine to possess when I was starving through graduate school.

What reason did I have to feel depressed? He asked me.

I couldn't answer. I only knew that I was. "You'd know when YOU turn 40," I said.

He said, "Maybe."

Then we went into nostalgia mode and became reminiscent on our days as graduate students. We had abandoned our life in China and come to U.S. to start all over. Life was anything but easy. We worked 60-hour weeks and lived on Top Ramen while trying to get through school as fast as we could. We had no idea

 I couldn't sleep that night. The next day I didn't go to work. Instead I drove around town and stopped at a bench where I sat.

what the future held for us. Curiously, amidst such materialistic "have-nots", hardship and uncertainty, I was optimistic and energetic. My life was full of happy moments and excitements.

"Perhaps you are depressed because now the future is here and you have nothing more to hope for," Jeff offered.

I choked. That really hit home.

My whole life I have been chasing one dream after another. I wanted to be loved and to love; I wanted to be independent; I wanted to immerse myself in a foreign culture; I wanted to be a US citizen. I have always had a goal to hope for, to work for, and to envision myself achieving.

I have attained all of that. I am not an ungrateful person. I love everything I have achieved in my life. I am thankful to my husband, my friends, my mentor, and everybody who helped me along the way. But now suddenly I want to complain about everything. Turning 40 isn't the only thing that bothers me. I complain about my long drive to work, my lack of ideas as to what to cook for dinner, my daughter's babysitter. . . . The list goes on.

What has happened to me?

I couldn't sleep that night. The next day I didn't go to work. Instead I drove around town and stopped at a bench where I sat. I sat and let my mind wander. I realized that I am depressed because I have become so grounded that I forgot how to dream. My life has become a grind with no destination.

What if I take on some new challenges? What if I lift myself off the ground and take a new flight, away from reality and into the garden of my imagination? What might I find there? That was the day when I found the secret of happiness: Never stop imagining the impossible; never stop going after your dreams.

Fast forward 10 more years, I have ventured upon many things I'd never thought I had in me: digital art, writing, public speaking, and even new responsibilities at work. This year I am turning 50. I am feeling full of life and optimism, more so than ever before. In fact, I even enjoy my look better. I have found new flowers to admire and new fruits to harvest in my garden of imagination.

Indeed, hope sprouts where we take a flight with our imagination and imagination injects happiness into our life.

Zee Gorman (zeegorman.blogspot.ca), *born in Southern China during the Cultural Revolution (both her parents were exiled to the countryside for being "intellectuals"), was raised within layers of political and cultural confines. Yet her love for literature gave wings to a life that is very different from what it is destined to be. She has written short stories, poems, and essays, and is mildly published in China. Her quest for a better life eventually led to her migration to the United States where she completed two Master's Degrees. Today, Zee Gorman lives in Northern California with her husband and her daughter. By night she is a writer, an artist, a crafter... whatever she imagines herself to be and by day she has a career in IT management.*

Why I Love Running in the Rain

By JOHN MCLAUGHLIN (Bathurst, New Brunswick) 19 July 2011

They call me a Clydesdale, because I like to run and I weigh over 200 pounds. As Clydesdales go, I'd say I'm a fairly large specimen. Sometimes I think a body like mine wasn't meant for running. My legs constantly feel heavy, my back end droops behind me, and sometimes I swear I make the earth shake under the relentless pounding of my old size twelves.

But still, I run. Despite the shin splints and tired knees, despite the middle aged gut that won't respond to all that exercise, and despite the laboured breathing and general fatigue, I still run.

I've clopped along through four marathons in my day, enduring the grinding joints and aching feet, all in the name of some strange personal goal. I've sworn that each marathon would be my last: that I'd toss the old running shorts and t-shirts in the trash rather than the laundry hamper.

But still, I run.

These days, I'm training for my fifth marathon... my last one, I've been telling myself. I get tired of experiencing the runner's low. It might be easier if every now and again my endorphins would rush, but that never seems to happen to me. My body and soul just never elevate themselves to runner's nirvana.

Well, almost never.

This morning I hit the road early, determined to get my dreaded weekly long run behind me before I'd have the chance to talk myself out of it. Then half way through, miracle of miracles, it happened: it started to rain, to pour rain, and all at once I got the high.

The harder it rained, the higher I got! It came down so hard that my feet were fully covered in water as it rushed down the street in search of a drain pipe. At once, my body was cooled, the aches washed away. I ran faster, with greater strides, not to rush home, but to feel the wild splashing beneath my feet, and the lowering

INSPIRING HOPE — ONE STORY AT A TIME

of my body temperature as the rain soaked my head. I literally galloped: bounding, splashing, leaping joyfully like a son-of-a-Clysdesdale, no longer the old horse I'd thought I'd become.

When I run in the rain, I understand why real runners do it. In the rain, you see, I am a real runner, and it is those precise moments that cause me to think that maybe, just maybe, there's one more marathon left in this big old Clydesdale.

"Send 'er down!" I heard myself exclaim, as I ran playfully through the torrent, rounding the bend onto our little cul-de-sac which was now filling up like a community wading pool. My wife was reading on our front verandah, protected from the very rain that I couldn't get enough of. She looked at me the way my mother once did, her expression enough to warn me not to track all that water onto her nice, clean floors. I sat down on the steps, noticing how the rain was letting up, how the sunlight was cutting through the clouds like prisms from Heaven. I smiled at her.

"Now that…" I said, peeling my wet shirt away from my skin. "That, my dear, was a really great run!"

John McLaughlin is Deputy Minister at the New Brunswick Department of Education & Early Childhood Development. As a former teacher and superintendent of schools, he believes the highest goal of education should be to nurture in students a sense of goodness, so they graduate from high school equipped not just with strong academic skills, but also a desire to contribute positively to the world, and to care for its people. John and his wife, Cathy, have four grown daughters, and they live in Bathurst on New Brunswick's beautiful northeastern coast.

Kids Do Say the Darndest Things

By GARY DOI (Penticton, British Columbia) 20 June 2012

Whoever said that laughter does for emotional health what exercise does for the body knew what they were talking about. Laughter can add moments of brightness to even the darkest days. It can put a smile on your face—sometimes, when you most need it.

Laughter is a powerful antidote. It builds resilience and creates hopefulness. Or, think of it this way, a hearty laugh (or a gentle chuckle) is good for the soul.

As a former school superintendent, I've worked with plenty of students, teachers and principals so I "own" a cupboard full of material. Some of the stories I treasure most are the light-hearted moments and situations with children. As Art Linkletter and Bill Cosby both proclaimed—Kids say the darndest things!

Here are a few schoolhouse anecdotes to tickle your funny bone!

***

One day while observing a class of students lining up for an assembly I overheard this curious conversation between two grade 6 children.

"Do you know who that is?" said one of the boys looking in my direction.

"That's the Superintendent," replied his friend.

"Right. Do you know he can fire a school principal!" he said dramatically.

"Really?" said the other. "Wow... imagine what he could do to us students!"

***

A kindergarten child was sent to the principal's office for not listening and not following directions in class.

INSPIRING HOPE – ONE STORY AT A TIME

The principal spoke to the young lad about his behavior but the six year old had others things on his mind. He gazed about the room and then, out of the blue said, "Must be nice to be principal."

The principal smiled, his mind racing with all kinds of thoughts. Was it nice to be principal? "Nice" wasn't the exact word he'd use — especially on days he was overworked and overstressed. But he liked the job. The only better job he'd ever had was when he played in a rock band but that was years ago. Back then he was slim, young and his hair was long. Today, he was middle-aged, out-of-shape and had a horseshoe-shaped fringe of hair. So, what would he say to this inquisitive child? All that came to mind was this —

"If you work hard," he said, "you may grow up to be a principal one day."

To which the child impulsively blurted out, "If I was a principal, would I have to get a haircut like yours?"

***

Spike was a pet lizard the children of the school adored. One day, however, someone noticed that Spike's skin colour had changed from dark brown to black; he had stopped breathing and lay collapsed in his glass container.

Spike had given up the ghost. The news hit the children hard, leaving many in tears.

During the recess break when most of the children were outside, the teacher decided to dispose of the dead animal. However — as she reached inside the container — Spike suddenly lifted his head. That startled the teacher so much she changed skin colour, stopped breathing and almost collapsed.

The news of Spike's resurrection (it was Easter time, after all) spread quickly as a young boy ran around the playground like the town crier shouting, "It's a miracle! It's a miracle! Spike lives! Spike lives!"

***

Charlie (not his real name) was a grade four student and a chronic visitor to the principal's office. Charlie struggled academically and had difficulty getting along with the other children. Mostly, though, Charlie was sent to the office for saying the F word in class — the actual F word.

Mrs. C, a dedicated, caring and compassionate principal, tried various strategies to dissuade Charlie from using such colourful language. She talked with him about how upsetting it was for the other students, discussed the importance of having school rules for bad language, tried to make connections with Charlie's outside interests (which were limited) and even had a special meeting with Charlie's mother. That's when Mrs. C realized the scope of the problem. During the meeting, Charlie's mother frequently dropped the F-bomb to describe her views of the school and her son.

The end of the school term was nearing, and Mrs. C publicly announced her retirement in the school newsletter. One day, as Charlie was leaving the principal's office, he stopped at the door and asked her a question.

"Is it true you are going, Mrs. C?" said Charlie.

"That's right, Charlie," she said. "I've worked a lot of years, and I am going to retire next month."

Charlie didn't say anything for a moment. He lowered his head a little, dropped his voice to a whisper and said, "I'll miss you Mrs. C. You're the best F___ principal I've ever had."

Gary Doi served as Superintendent of Schools for eighteen years in three school districts in British Columbia. Previous to that, he was a teacher, school administrator and university lecturer. He created the magazine blog, "A Hopeful Sign" (ahopeful-sign.com), as he believes there is no greater force for creating change than hope.

Of Geese and Men

By RICK COGBILL (Summerland BC, Canada) 11 October 2011

"So this goose walks into a bank and says..."

"Hold it." I took a sip of my decaf double Grande non-fat extra-dry cappuccino. "Is this that old joke where the goose wants a safety deposit box to store its golden egg?"

Buck scowled down at his boringly Tall Americano. "You just ruined my punch line."

I shrugged. "It's not my fault your jokes are stale."

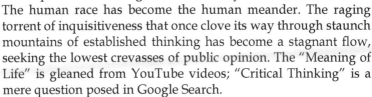

People are so unimaginative these days. The human race has become the human meander. The raging torrent of inquisitiveness that once clove its way through staunch mountains of established thinking has become a stagnant flow, seeking the lowest crevasses of public opinion. The "Meaning of Life" is gleaned from YouTube videos; "Critical Thinking" is a mere question posed in Google Search.

Take my friend Buck (please). Just once, I'd like to hear him spout a far-out yarn, a dynamic barn-burning tale so unbelievable that it might actually be true. Like what happened to me the other day, when this goose came walking into the bank and...

No, I'm not making this up.

16th in line at the Saturday morning bank teller, coffeeless and pitiful, my weekend was doomed to mediocrity when suddenly the glass doors slid open and in waddled a goose on a leash. Thankfully it was wearing a diaper.

Naturally,I tried to ignore it. Like most humourists, I suffer a marked lack of social skills, but at least I know that it's impolite to stare. Yet every blessed soul around me was not only staring, but hauling out cell phones and taking video. Some even had the audacity to converse with the owner, asking questions about goose husbandry and the early childhood development issues of goslings. I was appalled.

But my point here is not the goose in the bank lobby, but rather the goose owner who brought it there. I admired her imagination, her quest for uniqueness — in short, her zest for life. After all, this was not something you saw every day, and furthermore, it didn't happen by accident. This was an example of intentional life.

She had bought a gosling (or perhaps had it hatched), raised it in close contact with humans, and then leash-trained it to be quietly led along crowded city sidewalks. Here was a woman not shy of attention, who invited comment from strangers, and who obviously didn't give a honk about public opinion. There was passion and purpose in her life choices, and whether you're a goose lover or not, you couldn't help but admire her creativity. Should she ever run for public office, she'll certainly have my vote.

"So you don't like my jokes?" Buck's question dragged me back to the unfortunate present. "What's wrong with them?"

"They lack imagination," I said. "No, let me rephrase that... *you* lack imagination. I mean, look at the coffee you drink."

His eyes narrowed. "Well, I could've ordered a solo Venti two-pump white mocha soy extra foam two Splenda Misto with Sumatra."

"So why didn't you?"

"Because it's all a joke." He jerked his thumb at the coffee counter. "One of your barista buddies even admitted that. 'It's just the illusion of choice,' he said. 'It's all just tiny differences — extra hot, no foam, non-fat — but it's all the same.'" Buck took a sip of his drink. "Them were his exact words."

The thought of Buck doing research on specialty coffee was a shocker. "You mean you actually interviewed someone?"

He shrugged. "Naw, I saw it on YouTube."

I rest my case.

Now, don't get me wrong; one day I hope Buck does in fact become a free thinker, but not just yet. Let's face it; some friends you keep around just to make yourself look good.

Rick Cogbill is a Canadian author and humor columnist living in the beautiful Oka-nagan Valley in southern British Columbia. His popular column, The Car Side has been running monthly in automotive trade magazines for over 15 years. His hilarious book, *A Fine Day for a Drive* is available online at *www.thecarside.com*. Rick is also the Director and Founder of Mercy Tech Mission, a non-profit group dedicated to relieving poverty by bringing skills training to Africa (mercytechmission.com).

A River Runs Through Me

By BRUCE MASTERMAN (High River, Alberta) 16 July 2011

"Eventually, all things merge into one, and a river runs through it. The river was cut by the world's great flood and runs over rocks from the basement of time. On some of the rocks are timeless raindrops. Under the rocks are the words, and some of the words are theirs. I am haunted by waters."

- Norman Maclean

On a bookshelf in my home office, under a framed original Jack Cowin line drawing of a brown trout, sit two vintage brass fly-fishing reels, three-inch-square glass paperweight with a rainbow-hued Garry salmon fly imbedded in it, and an empty, slightly tacky tin that once contained a sugary confection called Trout Tin Fisher-Mints. "Don't get caught with fish breath!" admonishes the script-type lettering on the tin.

But these items are merely the supporting cast. They aren't the most important things on the shelf.

That honour belongs to an oval, seven-inch-long flat rock that has been rubbed smooth by years, perhaps centuries, of being washed by running water, either a river or creek. It appears to have come "from the basement of time".

On this rock, my wife, Karen, has lovingly and meticulously reproduced, in fine calligraphy printed with black marker, the touching passage that crowns this column, like rich ice cream atop a blandish-tasting cone.

Iowa-born writer Norman Maclean wrote those mantric words in his famous novella *A River Runs Through It*, published in 1976. That was 16 years before Robert Redford turned it into an iconic movie starring Brad Pitt. The movie took fly-fishing from the myth of being a sport of tweed-wearing elitist sportsmen to its broader reality as a life-defining activity pursued by preachers, university students and, yes, even gambling, devil-may-care newspapermen with a thirst for good whiskey.

Suddenly, everyone wanted to learn to fly-fish just like Brad Pitt, to inject some balance into their hectic lives, and in the process perhaps slow down life's roller coaster to a more manageable pace. They wanted fly-fishing to help them find a better place, either physically or metaphorically.

I'd been fly-fishing for many years when A River Runs Through It hit the silver screen. I was already one of the so-called converted. But the movie, and then the book (I saw it before I read it), helped open my eyes to how others see the activity that had become my passion, and the people who pursue it. Suddenly, fly-fishing took on a near-mystical quality for me.

Anyone who has ever done it for any duration knows that fly-fishing is about a lot more than just catching fish. If Lance Armstrong were to write a book about the sport, he'd probably call it "It's Not About the Fish."

Oh sure, we catch fish, sometimes lots of fish, sometimes big fish and sometimes little fish. But there also are times when we

 Anyone who has ever done it for any duration knows that fly-fishing is about a lot more than just catching fish.

don't catch any fish.

Quite frankly, that's okay too.

It's okay because we're out in special places, beautiful places, usually away from crowds of people and always away from our desks, our volunteer and work obligations, the everyday pressures—the things that help define who we are but which often feel overwhelming.

It's okay because we're meeting the fish in their natural element, not ours. We are feeling the strong, surging current rush against our bodies, challenging us to stay upright, refreshing us, infusing us with energy and life itself.

It's okay because we are hoping to unlock the secret of the water that day, to find out what insect the trout are taking and to try to match that bug with the imitations in our fly boxes. It's part science, part crapshoot, a combination of gut feeling, experience and educated case.

It's okay because the line feels cool and smooth as it runs through our fingers, the thin plastic-coated thread the only physical connection between us, the water and, if we're lucky, the fish. The mere act of casting is tonic for the soul.

It's okay because we're watching dainty gray dippers flit from rock to rock, occasionally diving into the water in search of an insect.

But, when the magic happens, when a fish actually takes our offered fly, it all comes together, initially making us feel delighted surprise, then excitement followed by anxiety that the fish might get away before we're ready. If it does slip the hook, we enter a fantasy world of speculation and exaggeration.

And when we finally gently slip our hands around the body of the fish – trout, salmon or other – we feel joy and, inexplicably, sometimes even sadness because that is yet another experience we've had, and we're not sure how many more we've been allotted.

That fish—every fish—becomes preserved in our memory banks, there to withdraw whenever our spiritual beings are in

 For a brief time, we become part of rivers, their riffles, rapids, long and mysteriously-deep reaches, quiet pools and side channels.

need of a lift.

Fly-fishers come to view rivers as living, breathing entities. We become like the rocks on the river bottom, the whispering words, the river's story.

For a brief time, we become part of rivers, their riffles, rapids, long and mysteriously-deep reaches, quiet pools and side channels. We share them with the birds, animals and fish that live there, and sometimes even feel their often-chilly lifeblood when we take a dunking, on purpose or by accident.

We know their promise. We sometimes become discouraged that we can't unlock their secrets. We remember when we have caught fish but mainly remember when a fish has beaten us at our own game.

We resent ourselves for doing bad things to rivers, and we try to be hopeful for their futures and for ours.

We become, as Norman Maclean so poetically described, haunted by them.

And that is a good thing.

Bruce Masterman (brucemasterman.com) is an award-winning Alberta writer, book author, photographer, magazine assignment editor and college journalism instructor with a passion for conservation and almost anything outdoorsy. He contributes to various magazines, including Outdoor Canada, The Conservator, West, Reader's Digest and several others. Bruce is the author of two nonfiction books – Heading Out: A Celebration of the Great Outdoors in Calgary and Southern Alberta, and Paradise Preserved: The Ann and Sandy Cross Conservation Area – and has contributed to five others.

A Magical Moment

By GARY DOI (Penticton, British Columbia) 24 May 2011

Frank Leahy may be best known as the National Fiddle Champion who inherited the violin of Don Messer, Canada's defining icon of folk music during the 1960s. Along with that honour, Frank Leahy holds exclusive rights to the Don Messer name and image.

A number of years ago, Frank Leahy was touring and performing in local schools and needed a place to stay as his accommodation arrangements had not worked out. So I volunteered to have him live with my family for three days. Thankfully I did or else the following sequence of events would likely have not occurred.

One evening, over dinner conversation, Frank asked if I knew of a special place on the Northwest Coast I would recommend for a school performance. I told him about Hartley Bay, an isolated First Nations fishing village (population 200) accessible only by seaplane and boat and located at the mouth of Douglas Channel about 400 miles north of Vancouver, BC. They had boardwalks instead of roadways and an elementary school that was the pride of the village.

Frank was immediately interested so I wrote him a letter of introduction to give to School Principal Ernie Hill. I had worked with Ernie years before and knew that he would warmly welcome Frank to the school and community.

And that was it. Or, so I thought.

Six months passed.

One day as I was driving down the Vancouver Island highway, I heard Frank Leahy on the radio discussing the release of his new album. Near the end of the nationally-broadcast interview, he was asked the question: Of all the places you've performed on your tour, was there one place that really stood out? He said there was... it was a village called Hartley Bay.

I pulled over to the side of the road to listen to his story.

After performing for an appreciative school audience, Frank said he went outside to take in the cool ocean breeze and the spectacular beauty of the autumn colours. As he was standing there, an elderly native woman approached him as she had heard about the school performance.

She asked if he knew the Don Messer song called "The Hon-

 He rested it on his shoulder, reached for the bow and gently ran it across the bridge, making a couple of soulful notes.

eymoon Waltz."

Frank said he did.

She explained that "The Honeymoon Waltz" was the song she and her husband danced to at their wedding reception decades ago. She said she'd love to hear that song again as her husband had recently passed away.

Frank told her he'd be pleased to play that song. Even more so, he said — to her great surprise and delight — he would play the song on Don Messer's violin.

He unlocked the black carrying case and removed the precious instrument. He rested it on his shoulder, reached for the bow and gently ran it across the bridge, making a couple of soulful notes.

Then he played.

It was magical. The mountain breeze carried the sweet violin sounds amongst the tall cedars and throughout the little coastal village. The music captivated her. Past memories flooded her mind and she could not hold back the tears.

After the interview ended, I sat in my car a while longer trying to take in what I had just heard. It seemed so surreal, so mystical. Like a dream within a dream.

Call it luck, coincidence or karma… a lot of things had to line up for this moment to occur.

Gary Doi *served as Superintendent of Schools for eighteen years in three school districts in British Columbia. Previous to that, he was a teacher, school administrator and university lecturer. He created the magazine blog, "A Hopeful Sign" (ahopeful-sign.com), as he believes there is no greater force for creating change than hope.*

PART 2: THE TRAVELLER SEES

"The traveler sees what he sees, the tourist sees what he has come to see." - Gilbert K. Chesterton

A Lifetime of Adventure — The Vogel Family

By NANCY SATHRE-VOGEL (Between North & South Poles) 23 Nov 2011

What was your moment—THE MOMENT? That is the question. What was the moment when you knew you wanted more out of life? When it suddenly became clear and you knew, deep down in your heart, that you weren't cut out for the normal drill.

When you knew you wanted to live a life designed by you, not by someone else. What was your moment?

As I think back through my life I realize I've had a lot of those moments, but I'll reach way back and consider the very first one.

I was sixteen. I lived like all sixteen-year-old kids in Boise, Idaho did. I went to school in the morning and attended football games in the evenings. I helped at the local hospital as a candy striper. I was involved in Girl Scouts and our church youth group.

Everybody I knew lived much like me and, I figured, everybody around the world lived much like me. When I watched National Geographic shows about some far-flung island in Indonesia where people wore funny costumes and painted their faces, I figured that happened hundreds of years ago. That wasn't today. Today, of course, everybody lived like I did.

Then my parents took us kids to Mexico for the Christmas holidays

I remember walking down the street in wide-eyed amazement

at how different things were. People in Mexico didn't live like I did back in Boise, Idaho. They ate different food; they lived in different houses; they wore different clothes. It was new, exciting, and exotic.

One scene from that trip is forever etched in my mind. That day we were walking along the street in Mexico City when we saw a street performer. My eyes widened as I watched him shoot flames from his mouth. They were huge! Six-foot-long tongues of fire shot out in front of him! It was wild. Exciting. Exotic. Different. People didn't stand on the street corner and shoot flames out of their mouths in Boise, Idaho.

As I watched him spit fire I drew nearer and nearer. It— HE—was fascinating beyond anything I'd ever experienced.

I wanted to drink it all in…every aspect of this wonderful new thing I was seeing. I never wanted to forget the wonder of it all.

My flame thrower walked over to a small bottle he kept near him, took off the top, and took a big swig. And I saw him gag. He

 All of a sudden, the flame thrower's show took on a different light. The flames, I now understood, weren't the mystical, magical things I had imagined them to be.

gamely forced it off and set fire to his mouth once again.

All of a sudden, the flame thrower's show took on a different light. The flames, I now understood, weren't the mystical, magical things I had imagined them to be. They were work. A necessary evil to put food on the table for his children at home. The flame thrower—MY flame thrower—came out here to this street corner every single day and poured kerosene in his mouth. And he gagged. Over and over and over. He did it to survive.

Mexico no longer seemed quite so exotic. It didn't seem so magical. It seemed poor and desperate. When I saw local artisans painstakingly cutting silver or potters churning out hundreds of clay figurines they sold for a pittance, I wondered if I could somehow make a difference. I was only one person; a child no less, but I was one.

The stage had been set.

A few weeks later I stumbled into our house in Boise after a long flight home. As sixteen-year-olds are wont to do, I flipped on the TV and relaxed into my favorite position on the floor. An advertisement for the Peace Corps came on.

I watched those images flash before my eyes. Life in a small village in Africa; volunteers helping build water systems; teachers in classrooms filled with eager young eyes.

I made a decision that day. As soon as I could, I would enter the Peace Corps. I would be one of those people who made a difference in the world. I would do what I could to help others less fortunate than I.

Eight years later that decision came to fruition. I graduated from college and entered the Peace Corps. I lived in a small Honduran village and worked with local teachers setting up Special Education programs for handicapped children, and I knew I was making a difference. It was a small contribution, but it was MY contribution.

So that was it — my moment in time. The moment that changed my life. The moment I made the decision to live a life less ordinary and follow my heart. That decision has led me around the world a time or two since then, but I will be forever grateful to my parents for taking me to Mexico that year. My parents who opened my eyes to a great big world out there.

And I'm thankful for my flame thrower for teaching me that although we may be different on the surface, underneath it all we're all the same.

What was YOUR moment?

Teachers John Vogel and Nancy Sathre Vogel (familyonbikes.org) *describe themselves as a normal, everyday, American family who happens to follow their dreams and chase rainbows. John, Nancy and their two children (Daryl and Davy) are modern-day explorers who learned early to live life to the fullest, to grab life by the horns and enjoy the ride. Together, they have pedaled bicycles 20,000 miles through fifteen countries. John and Nancy have published four books documenting their exciting adventures: Changing Gears, Twenty Miles Per Cookie; What Were We Thinking? And Bicycle Touring with Children.*

Following in the Steps of Emperors

By FRANCISCO LITTLE (Tai Shan, China) 27 September 2011

"The world is small," said Confucius. When he made that comment he was standing 1,545 meters above sea level on the top of Tai Shan (Mount Tai). When I stood in the same spot, I wondered if the great sage had a premonition about globalization, or he just marveled at the bird's eye view.

I lost count of the steps after 30 minutes. The part of my brain that switches off when I do anything strenuous signaled shut down and my feet moved metronomically. I kept telling myself I was following in the footsteps of 72 emperors, Confucius and even Chairman Mao himself. Suddenly the phrase 'one step at a time' took on a whole new meaning.

China's most sacred mountain has many stories to tell. Jutting out of the flat plains between the cities of Tai'an, Jinan and Zibo in Shandong Province, most Chinese have it down as a 'must climb' during their lifetime, irrespective of religious beliefs. Tai Shan's fame grew from the fact that in the past an emperor's first action after ascending to the throne was to make the arduous trek up to the summit and perform rituals and make sacrifices to heaven and earth.

Today the common folk that brave the almost 7000 step climb come to make their own blessings for fertility, long life, health or good fortune. Tai Shan has deep Taoist connections, with temples built into the mountain at all levels, where climbers burn incense and place metal locks in the hope of securing their future. Being included in the UNESCO world heritage list in 1987 has only added to the numbers of the many who make the pilgrimage.

Pausing for breath near a holy cave surrounded by stone inscriptions, I heard the familiar "hello, hello" greeting given to foreigners and turned to see what looked like a mountain man emerging from the shadowed entrance. His green army trench coat hung on an emaciated frame, long gray hair framing a face set off by eyes that looked clean through me. He beckoned me in, and never being short on curiosity I followed. The entrance eventually opened out into a smallish cave deep in the mountain, clouded with incense smoke and desperately cold. In the light of four fat red candles he motioned me to sit on a stone seat and proceeded to tell me my fortune. I sat, nodded appreciatively and left 20 minutes later, senses in a daze. I tried to press 50 yuan into his calloused hand but he waved me off, refusing payment.

The blue sky looked bluer now and I turned back to wave at my soothsayer but he had slunk back into the mountain. How did he know those things, I wondered? A bell echoed across the mountain, its deep sound seeming to come from the summit. I lifted my feet again.

The sense of where you are takes a while to sink in on Tai Shan. Having heard the stories about how poets, writers and

Pausing for breath near a holy cave surrounded by stone inscriptions, I heard the familiar "hello, hello" greeting given to foreigners and turned to see what looked like a mountain man emerging from the shadowed entrance.

artists headed for the mountain whenever they were in need of inspiration, and seeing the evidence all around me, in the form of thousands of inscribed stone tablets and cliff sculptures, the concentration of energy is palpable. It's the same feeling I had at Machu Picchu, the sacred Inca City in Peru.

A famous Chinese saying says, "Scaling Tai Shan makes one feel superior to the whole world," as it creates a feeling of regal dignity and imperial majesty. I think it makes you feel more connected to the ordinary things around you. Pausing at scenic spots with names like Azure Cloud Temple, Peak for Viewing the Sun and Mid-heaven Gate is a reminder that anyone can connect with nature and its power, irrespective of your station in life.

The last 2000 steps are almost vertical and continuous like a long chiseled granite ribbon. Small stalls selling trinkets, cucumber and tomatoes are dotted in the recesses. Stop to suck in crisp air and platoons of touts accost you to take photos, be carried up or just buy exorbitantly priced bottles of water. It's as if they have psychologically figured out that when you are at your weakest, it's the best time to sell anything. It works, and I watched people succumbing purely to be left in peace afterwards.

When the last waterfalls and oddly shaped pines and cypresses have given way and you look up, exhausted, at the red gate on the summit, it's a good feeling. A small village has been built on the flat section at the top where climbers can stop for tea, have a meal

After all, when we overcome challenges we earn the privilege to write our own story.

or spend the night in the hopes of catching the famed sunrise.

I went in search of the bell and found it on the 1st floor of a rickety tower jutting out from the west cliffs. The bell warden urged me to ring it. I held the ropes and closed my eyes to make a wish. As I was about to swing the wooden pole he stopped me. "10 yuan, 10 yuan," he said. I put my wish on hold, paid up and struck, shattering the sound of silence.

Outside on Jade Emperor Peak, the Temple of the God lay a calf-cramping 9 kilometers away, at the foot of the mountain. If, as the Chinese say, the climb up symbolizes your life, then the blank stele erected here made sense I thought. After all, when we overcome challenges we earn the privilege to write our own story.

Francisco Little (franciscolittle.com) is a much traveled South African born writer, photographer and artist, who grew up in Rhodesia, now Zimbabwe, where he studied Fine Art and Philosophy. He currently works as managing editor of a current affairs magazine and resides between Johannesburg, South Africa and Beijing, China. Francisco believes that in all aspects of life it is important to Trust the Process.

Will I Have to Wear a Burqa?

By CATHERINE SUNDHER (Abu Dhabi, UAE) 07 July 2011

Will I have to wear a *burqa*? That certainly was a question I wondered about before moving to the Middle East.

As I truly embraced the freedoms and opportunities that "my western world" had to offer, this was definitely not something I planned on doing. For years, I had absorbed horrendous stories of religious fanaticism, injustices, and terror that extremists were inflicting around the globe. I'd come to believe, women wearing a *burqa* symbolized powerlessness and despair. Not so.

In the UAE, burqa refers to a "falcon-wing" shaped face covering that is painted or dyed gold, then rubbed until very shiny. Originally, its purpose was to reflect the sun from the faces of women working in the fields. Now only a handful of older Bedouin women continue to wear them. More often though, *burqa* refers to a head to toe poncho type garment with small slits or mesh around the eyes; this is commonly worn in Afghanistan.

In this sovereign state, what most women choose to wear is called an *abaya* (neck to toe black robe) and *sheela* (headscarf). Covering their 'ornaments' (body and hair) in public makes an important statement of their faith and by being black in color, allows for the fabric to be ultra sheer yet not see-through. In order to visit the Grand Mosque, all women are provided with and required to wear the traditional *abaya* and *sheela*.

Among Arab nations, Abu Dhabi is definitely one of the more tolerant and progressive. It's an Islamic country deeply rooted in its customs, yet open-minded to western influences and ideas. Islam's teachings and practices affect not only what a Muslim eats, drinks and wears, but it's a way of life.

For the new generation of Emirati women, culture and tradition remain a top priority yet their fervor for worldwide fashion trends is evident. Black abayas on the cutting edge of design ensure their modesty while underneath, theatrical make-up and bold fashion statements are the norm — not in a club, but at the shopping malls! In the thousands of windowless saloons, a staggering $870 million was spent last year (in UAE) in the name of beauty. Adorned with designer handbags, heels and oversize sunglasses, many resemble fashion models — certainly not oppressed women.

After being here for many months, Emirati women still continue to be a huge mystery to me. Homes where large extended families live and socialize are shielded from prying eyes by high walls and heavy drapes earnestly guarding their privacy. They rarely attend public sporting or social events (especially if there's alcohol) and do not normally mingle with expats. Even for those in the work place, it's strictly "business".

Former US Senator Bill Frist (in his book A Heart to Serve) stated, "Education is the cornerstone of our community and our country". This certainly rings true in the UAE. The top priority for over 70% of young women is to attain a post-secondary education. After graduation, their challenge then lies with finding rewarding employment as not all families are open-minded. Fathers and husbands still hold legal authority as to whether daughters or wives can work and if so, preferably where they'll be minimal exposure to men. Much of the restriction and disparity comes from cultural traditions rather than Islam itself. Slowly, though, women are bridging the barriers of their traditional roles with modern ways of thinking, setting new standards for this region.

The winds of change are indeed sweeping across the Arab World. Some say, women are the key to Islam's modernization and here in the Gulf, they're making great strides as they move towards a more independent mindset. I'm hopeful, one day, all women will have "choice".

One step at a time.

Catherine Sundher is a West Coast girl who feels fortunate to call Victoria, British Columbia (Canada) as her "home-base". She's happily married to an educator and has two grown and independent sons. Curious by nature and with a perpetual desire for new challenges, Catherine has moved from the "Travel Industry to Design" with numerous stops along the way. As Gilbert Chesterson wrote, "Why Not" is a slogan for an interesting life.

Ignorance is Bliss

By FRANCISCO LITTLE (Beijing, China) 08 November 2011

I remember when I was growing up my parents would often tell my sisters and me, "Finish your dinner-people in China are starving." Well historically we all know that this is true, and there was a tragic period when people in China were starving. But we can safely say that those days are gone. What hasn't gone, it seems, is the perception that there is still very little food in the motherland.

I have just returned from a holiday to South Africa and was once again amazed by the level of ignorance that exists about life in China. Being born and bred in Cape Town, arguably the world's most beautiful city, I am still greeted with nods of disbelief from people I bump into, that I have actually gone to live "over there" in China. "How could you swap paradise for pollution?" they wail.

"It's so far," say others. "What made you make such a drastic change in your life?" Despite looking healthy, I am always asked the most ridiculous questions, the most common of which is "Is there enough food 'over there'?" It is at this point that I feel like shipping the lot of them "over here" to see for themselves not only how much food there actually is, but how much of it gets wasted. Anyone who has lived in China for a while will have seen the vast quantities of meat, fish, vegetables and other edibles that adorn tabletops long after the last chopsticks have been cast aside. It's the host's duty to show his generosity in the form of an excess of everything and eating every last morsel, as would please a Western host, would be most insulting on these shores. I'm sure if I had to open a business whereby I collected all the leftovers of every restaurant in Beijing, I could be feeding half the world's poor, free, gratis, for nothing. If these leftovers are going to feed pigs and other livestock, they must be the best fed in the entire universe. The pendulum has swung the other way and where before there was nothing, it is now time to wallow in excess. All is not lost however, as I have recently noticed the introduction of a Chinese version of the doggie bag, with many diners now lugging home mounds of all those tasty bits that couldn't find their way into extended stomachs.

Despite the details of these lunches and dinners, my friends back in South Africa remain skeptical and always load me up with endless snack bars in case the food in Beijing should run out.

It's not only in the food stakes that my friends and family worry. "What about the language?" they chorus. "How will you communicate with people?" Here I have to admit that my Chinese language skills are nowhere near fluent, but I manage to get by. I assure my frowning friends that many Chinese people now have English language skills, in varying degrees, and being understood is not that much of a calamity. "No way" they mutter, "I would be too worried if there was an emergency and I couldn't make myself

 It's usually at this point that I consider there really are different kinds of people.

understood." Hearing this I thought to myself I would be worried in China whether I could be understood or not in an emergency. But then that would be contradictory, wouldn't it?

Ultimately most people I know back home just can't get their heads around how I live surrounded by so many people. "Isn't it irritating being bumped and shoved all the time?" or "How can you have any privacy?" they ask. To be honest I don't even notice being bumped and shoved. Maybe being 1.91 meters tall means I don't get bumped and shoved often. And if I want privacy I go into my apartment and lock the door.

It's usually at this point that I consider there really are different kinds of people. Some are adventurous, willing to experience other cultures and lifestyles despite the many perceived inconveniences. Others are ensconced in a time warp, trapped by their own fears and wedged in their own corners of ignorance. For these it's just too difficult to try something new and far easier to criticize and dismiss those who do.

As William Blake said, "In the universe, there are things that are known, and things that are unknown, and in between, there are doors," — however there is not enough evidence in all of creation to convince those who won't acknowledge that there is life and opportunity beyond one's comfort zone.

Francisco Little (franciscolittle.com) *is a much traveled South African born writer, photographer and artist, who grew up in Rhodesia, now Zimbabwe, where he studied Fine Art and Philosophy. He currently works as managing editor of a current affairs magazine and resides between Johannesburg, South Africa and Beijing, China. Francisco believes that in all aspects of life it is important to Trust the Process.*

A Walk on the Wild Side

By VALLI-L. FRASER-CELIN (Hoedspruit, South Africa) 22 November 2012

Living in Africa, I've been lucky enough to go on more game drives than I can count and I've definitely seen some amazing and wondrous things... from a vehicle. However, there is something really special about taking a walk on the wild side of the fence.

Suddenly, being at the mercy of Mother Nature and all her beautiful creatures has a way of really putting me in my place in the grand scheme of all things strong and unforgiving. On foot, all of my senses become heightened and I am suddenly very aware that a well-camouflaged lion hiding behind the next bush could easily take me out or that walking into a herd of elephants when the wind is not in your favour can be potentially life threatening.

Fear and exhilaration mix together but when I feel the ground beneath my feet, the wind on my face, and hear the rustling of dry grass as I walk through the bush I feel alive and there is nowhere else I'd rather be. The singsong of birds, the sound of hurried hooves hitting the dry earth as wildebeest and impala sense our arrival, and the musky, earthy smell of elephant grounds me in this place, this moment in time.

Looking down at my feet, I see tracks and trails made by thousands of different animals and I am reminded how we are far from being alone, far from being the most important living being on this great planet. We are only a thin thread of an intricate web encompassing all creatures, big and small, dangerous and unassuming, a web we must take great care of before it disintegrates.

The bush I walk through here in South Africa is a home to all of these amazing and interesting creatures and the game trails we follow have been leading them throughout this vast country for millions of years.

I am so thankful that they allow me to be here, that they share their wonderful world with me and that they let me walk the paths they've created. It is truly a privilege for me to be able to set foot in this untamed, wild land.

Valli-Laurente Fraser-Celin (whereisvalli.wordpress.com) grew up in Montreal, Quebec, Canada and currently lives in Guelph, Ontario pursuing her PhD in Geography where she is examining human-African wild dog relations in Botswana. In 2010, Valli volunteered at the Southern African Wildlife College in the Kruger National Park in South Africa for over a year. Valli is passionate about how people and wild animals coexist in shared landscapes in both Africa and Canada.

ALMS on Beggar's Road

By FRANCISCO LITTLE (Himachal Pradesh, India) 10 September 2011

(Wikipedia defines "alms" or almsgiving as a religious rite which involves giving materially to another as an act of religious virtue.)

Even though being confronted by beggars in India is as commonplace as the sun rising and setting each day, there is something rather disconcerting about walking a three-kilometre long gauntlet of continuous outstretched hands and pleading eyes. Cloth wrapped impoverished hopefuls line both sides of a dirt road, sitting patiently — waiting for the one day of the year that historically lines their pockets with more than dust.

June 15 — just another date for many around the world, but in the far north Indian mountain village of McLeod Ganj this is a very auspicious day. It is known as Saga Dawa Duchen, the anniversary that celebrates the birth, death and moment of enlightenment of Prince Siddhartha, the historical Buddha — and no village in the world has more connection with Buddha than this one, as it is the exiled home of Tibetan spiritual leader His Holiness the 14th Dalai Lama.

On this day Buddhists believe that any act of generosity, kindness and sacrifice takes on a special significance, and the merit that it brings one's own karma is multiplied 100000-fold. They prepare by saving their one and two rupee coins throughout the year, for the sole purpose of giving a coin to every outstretched hand or rattling tin cup.

I had ended up here by accident, having originally been on my way to climb the Dhauladhar mountain range, the outer edge of the Himalayas, that forms the backdrop to the village, and taken a detour that came out on the famous beggar's road. It's a narrow, muddy track that runs around the home and monastery of the Dalai Lama and then winds its way up to Mcleod Ganj, a former summer retreat village of British aristocracy.

I tried to put what I saw into perspective, but had a hard time dealing with simultaneous feelings of pity, compassion, shame and revulsion. The road seemed to murmur and each pair of sunken eyes pierced my conscience. There were just so many people and they looked so helpless.

I stopped to give a grubby mother holding her crying baby some money. She shook her cup without looking at me.

My good intentions were interrupted before I could let go of the coins.

"Don't give her money sir," a male voice called above the noise. "She's not a genuine beggar."

"What do you mean she's not a genuine beggar, she looks pretty destitute to me," I said turning to look at the man. He had one arm and a face ravaged by leprosy. He motioned me over to where he squatted.

"She works in Mumbai sir and is one of many people who just come here at this time of year to make extra money," he said.

He told me in the past years "real" beggars could count on collecting at least 400 rupees (R82) on June 15, which would see them

 "Namaste" he said placing his hands together gently. "The divine in me greets the divine in you and wishes you long life."

through perhaps two months. He said these unscrupulous people were reducing the "noble art" of begging to an "opportunistic free for all."

The woman was not impressed at the thought of losing out on my donation and let loose a stream of Hindi that was clearly designed to leave no doubt as to the origins and occupation of the man's mother. Her screams woke the baby, which howled its own protest.

On the left of the woman, a wild-eyed bearded friend/co-conspirator saw what was going down and joined in the vitriolic attack at not only my leper confidant, but clearly at me as well. Images flashed through my mind of being leapt upon by swarms of beggars and ripped limb from limb.

I decided it was time to be somewhere else, dropped a coin into the leper's cup and headed north. In front of me a family of

Tibetans were methodically handing out coins, seemingly basing the amount on the "condition" of the beggar.

I kept my head down and walked, avoiding any eye contact. It had started to rain. I was close to the end of the path when a soaked family of four called me over.

"Please sir we have only collected 25 rupees—we won't have enough to get to our next destination. The competition here is too fierce," said the father. His eyes registered no emotion, but the boy holding his hand offered a small smile.

"Where are you off to next?" I asked.

"Panthankhot," he said, naming the small train station town about 75 kms away.

I had just come from that direction and knew that he was telling the truth about the cost of the bus fare. I bent down to drop a note into his tin cup. He didn't register at first as there was no rattling of coins, then he looked down and saw the paper money.

"Namaste" he said placing his hands together gently. "The divine in me greets the divine in you and wishes you long life."

I nodded and watched as he rose with great dignity, and helped his frail wife and two children gather their meagre belongings. They were moving on—and it seemed a moment of great reflection.

Behind me the rattling of tin cups rose up above the sound of rain and I felt a deep sense of hope. I was moving on too.

Francisco Little (franciscolittle.com) is a much traveled South African born writer, photographer and artist, who grew up in Rhodesia, now Zimbabwe, where he studied Fine Art and Philosophy. He currently works as managing editor of a current affairs magazine and resides between Johannesburg, South Africa and Beijing, China. Francisco believes that in all aspects of life it is important to Trust the Process.

30 Days of Ramadan

By CATHERINE SUNDHER (Abu Dhabi, UAE) 09 August 2011

Excitement's in the air as 1.7 billion Muslims throughout the world celebrate the much revered and auspicious month of Ramadan. It begins with the crescent moon sighting, which this year was on August 1st (as per the Islamic lunar calendar) and for 30 days from sun-up to sun-down, Muslims fast every day; no smoking, no drinking, no eating—not even water or chewing gum! Even for us non-Muslims, in public, it's illegal not to adhere to these rules during daylight hours. Yet, during this time of intense physical discipline, self-denial and unrelenting daytime heat, it's a much anticipated and fondly embraced month.

In Muslim countries, extensive preparations take place for Ramadan. At night, boulevards glow with thousands of twinkling decorations, grocery stores are packed with shoppers stocking up on specialty items, newspapers and magazines are chalk full of "holiday deals" and special Ramadan TV shows, are huge hits. Lavish *iftar tents* hosting expensive nightly buffets surround major hotels, while at sunset, police and citizens can be seen distributing free *iftar meals* to passing citizens—one can't help, but get into the *"Spirit of Ramadan"*.

During this time, Muslims consciously shift their attention away from the busyness and concerns of "daily life" and instead, seriously focus on their "spiritual life". There's increased concentration on religious devotion, reflection and discovery, while reading the entire Quran is tradition and something most accomplish by month's end. Fasting cleanses and strengthens the body and mind, while experiencing hunger and thirst, reminds them to empathize and feel compassion for the poor. Any gain acquired through fasting and good deeds can easily be cancelled out by exercising bad habits such as gossip, greed or anger so they are not to be taken lightly.

Few people are exempt from fasting and from puberty on, it's compulsory for Muslims to participate. Mornings begin around 4:30 am, as everyone awakes to share and enjoy the morning *suhoor meal*; then, for fourteen plus hours nothing will pass their lips until dusk. Immediately following sunset prayer, the fast is traditionally broken with water and dates, followed by the much anticipated *iftar*. Everyone partakes in these mouth-watering feasts, at home, in hotels or for the many expat laborers, at various neighborhood mosques. A favorite element during Ramadan, are these "meal times" together.

The rhythm of life also dramatically alters; food and beverage establishments remain closed until dusk as do shops and malls in the afternoons. Finding a bank or post office open, seems to be a matter of hit and miss. "Night becomes day" as businesses stay open until the wee hours of the morning and people "out and about" fill the streets. These early mornings and late nights, make for some rather erratic sleep patterns and less productive work hours.

Ramadan climaxes with *Eid al-Fitr* (festival of fast-breaking).

 One can't help, but become somewhat nostalgic and a little bit sad, when the time arrives to bid Ramadan a fond farewell.

Official government/school holidays are far and few between here in the UAE, so this is a much anticipated and highly celebrated 3-day break. It's one of the rare occasions, when hundreds of thousands of laborers will also receive time off. Huge masses congregate in large open-air prayer grounds adorned in new clothes, sprayed with perfume, all waiting for special *Eid* prayers to be performed. Now it's time to celebrate, socialize and exchange gifts among family and friends.

For 30 extraordinary days and nights, everyone is more gracious, more giving and more kind. One can't help, but become somewhat nostalgic and a little bit sad, when the time arrives to bid Ramadan a fond farewell.

Until next time . . . Ramadan Kareem!

The Way to Santiago

By CHERINA HADLEY (Melbourne, Australia) 28 July 2011

With a UK and US release of Martin Sheen's latest movie *The Way* announced in April, I thought now would be as good a time as any to write about the Camino de Santiago.

No idea what I'm talking about? The Camino, or *The Way of St James*, is both an 780 km long ancient pilgrimage trail in Northern Spain and... something you should put on your travel 'to do' list right now!

You either like to walk, or you don't. If you like to walk, you will fall in love with the Camino. If you don't like to walk...you will fall in love with the Camino. Whilst it is undeniably a really bloody long walk and you are bound to develop a blister or two along with an entirely new and improved concept of pain, it is also about way more than just walking.

It's about an incredible sense of achievement. It's about strength, determination, courage and tolerance. It's about friendship and camaraderie. It is slow travel at its finest through one of the most stunning places in the world. It's about completely immersing yourself in a different culture. It's a wakeup call. (Oh, and it's also about eating divine tapas and drinking some of the best wine in the world—which is useful as you'll need *something* to ease the pain of walking so far every day!) And even if you try really hard not to let it, walking the Camino will inevitably change your way of looking at things.

The Camino has its historical base in Christianity and while I'm the first to admit that the tale has a few flaws, it goes a little something like this: St James was one of Jesus' best buddies back in the day and legend has it that after a stint of spreading the word in Spain, St James returned to Judea and ran into a little bad luck: he was beheaded! His Christian followers transported his martyred body in a stone boat (Yes, 'stone'! Did I mention that this story has flaws?) to Padron on the north coast of Spain and then carried him to the site of the modern city of Santiago. St James is now the Patron Saint of Spain and his remains are said to be housed within the cathedral in Santiago.

And so the pilgrimage began.

For a little more adventure, I highly recommend attempting this walk in the winter months. Walking the Camino in winter

 And even if you try really hard not to let it, walking the Camino will inevitably change your way of looking at things.

presents a series of different challenges and while the weather is incredibly unpredictable, it is a truly spectacular season to be in Northern Spain.

And, in case you are wondering, no you don't have to be religious or on some kind of neo-pagan spiritual quest to walk the Camino as a pilgrim. Over a hundred thousand people walk the Camino each year. On my last Camino I walked alongside both a die-hard atheist and a devout Catholic. Even the heathens amongst us will find some kind of spiritual side to the Camino—even if it is caused purely by the pain in your feet!

But don't just take my word for it. Have a look at the trailer for *The Way* for some inspiration. *The Way* is a fictional representation of one man's unexpected journey along the Camino. He makes the decision to walk the Camino after his son tragically dies on the first day of his own pilgrimage. (Don't let this put you off though — most people live to tell the tale… I promise!!)

Buen Camino.

Just a Walk in the Park

By FRANCISCO LITTLE (Beijing, China) 30 December 2011

One of the things I enjoy about living in Beijing in summer is the trip to work each morning. My day starts off with a seven-minute subway ride, three stops east from the financial district where I live.

I'm an early riser, so at 7 am there is not much movement about and the coaches are reasonably empty. The last word in this sentence is not often used to describe anything in China, so I'm savoring it.

Subway rides cost about US$0.25 and you can travel anywhere across the city for this price. Subway trains are clean, fast and run on time. And at this time of the morning they're empty.

Even at 7 am the temperature is in the mid-30s, with an uncomfortable coat of humidity hanging over the city, pinned in place by the incessant gray clouds of air pollution that prevent any glimpse of a blue sky.

Bird men of Muxidi Park

I get off at a stop called Muxidi and take a 30-minute walk north, passing through a public park on the way. It's the kind of experience that you want to repeat. The park is a sanctuary for senior citizens, who pour down from the surrounding hi-rise apartment blocks that characterize Beijing, to go through their time honored morning rituals.

At the entrance to the park are the `bird men'. Most people who imagine life in China will no doubt have an image somewhere in their minds of old, vest wearing men carrying bird cages about. Well, it really does happen.

There are usually about 30 bird men about, and by the time I get there many have already hung up their cylindrical bamboo cages amongst the trees. Each cage is brought, usually on the back of a tricycle, covered in white or blue cloth. The bottom of each cage is cleaned and then to the obvious delight of the occupants the cages are hung up.

Most of the birds are thrushes, larks and mynas and the combined singing volume can be heard almost two blocks away. Larks can imitate the sounds of other animals, as I found out when I thought there was a goat in the park one morning, only to find a bird producing pitch-perfect goat snorts.

Displaying birds is a vital part of urban Chinese park culture, particularly among the elderly, and dates back 2000 years. With the birds sorted, the men sit around shooting the breeze (or lack of it) and sucking on cigarettes, shirts rolled up to show their stomachs in that peculiar Chinese fashion of keeping cool, while watching the world go by. Some also form mahjong groups, loudly slapping down their ivory pieces in morning bonhomie. I guess for them it's a great way to begin the day in the company of their mates, and they just bring the birds along as an excuse.

Morning rituals

I walk on past the birds along a path that winds through cerise pink rose bushes. On my left a man in his pajamas hangs by his arms from a tree branch, like a large fruit, having a morning stretch. A vacant faced woman near him is busy slapping her body, beginning with her head, then chest, legs and back in a massage routine. Her loose-limbed movements belie her advanced years and each slap increases the wistful look on her wrinkled face. Flagellation is alive and well.

The dog brigade is a great showstopper. Middle-aged women kitted out in a various assortment of flesh revealing outfits gather in tight groups, heads bent, engaged in the latest juicy gossip. But they are not the main attraction here, that honor is left to the dogs. This is small-dog territory, and while there are several breeds on show, quite fittingly the Pekinese reigns supreme. The bulging-eyed, flowing-haired pooches prance and preen knowing they're being watched by passers by, to the obvious pride of their gaggling owners. The dogs sniff at my trouser leg as I pass. I do a side-step.

Passing the dog pool I stop and watch an eccentric fellow writing Chinese characters on the cement pathway. That in itself is odd, but get this—he's using a sponge tied to a broomstick as a brush, and water as ink! Even to an untrained eye like mine, the characters are beautifully formed. The idea apparently is a cheap way for the writer to practice his calligraphy, exercise his upper body and share words of wisdom with the community. As he writes every 7th character the first one fades… a great lesson in the transience of life.

Inspired I walk on, winding my way past benches where seated students pore over study notes and early morning lovers entwine in public cuddles. A gray-haired woman is busy arranging dis-counted clothing in a cart. She seems to move in time with the water sprinklers that bring life to the lawns and neat beds of flowers.

Fragile warriors…

A large area off the pathway is seemingly the practice ground for every martial art conceivable. I usually find an empty bench and watch the display from the sidelines, but if there were an entrance fee I'd gladly pay.

An elegant man, resplendent in white silk Chinese pajamas goes through a free flowing tai chi routine. His students are all ordinary folk on their way to work and follow his movements effortlessly. It's relaxing just to watch as bodies of all ages rise and dip in the warm air.

A group of elderly ladies nearby pierce the air softly with silver swords like gentle, fragile warriors, while their neighbors step and swirl, cracking open large red fans in trained synchronicity. My view is interrupted briefly by two ladies walking backwards, chatting at the top of their lungs, who stop to share their thoughts with an animated man spinning a large wooden reel, using a length of string and a lot of energy.

Everything is in motion. Even passers by seem to fall into a rhythm, absorbing the energy of others and for a few moments lightening the load. There is a sense of release to it all, like the saying "Dance like there is no one watching." It's the timeless part of China that embodies well-being. A need to nurture body, mind and spirit.

I get up reluctantly from my quiet repose and continue my journey to work. At the park exit I pass a smartly dressed businessman, leg stretched high and arms curled in a complicated tai chi movement. He's in his own world. His serene expression fades suddenly as a cell phone shrieks, demanding attention. He reaches into his jacket pocket retrieves the instrument and begins a loud conversation. His left leg is still stretched high and he retains his pose while talking.

Modern life meets morning work out. It's a wake up call. I head back into the carbon monoxide clouds of the noisy main street and am jostled by pedestrians rushing on the crowded street. Yin and yang. You've gotta love it.

Francisco Little (franciscolittle.com) is a much traveled South African born writer, photographer and artist, who grew up in Rhodesia, now Zimbabwe, where he studied Fine Art and Philosophy. He currently works as managing editor of a current affairs magazine and resides between Johannesburg, South Africa and Beijing, China. Francisco believes that in all aspects of life it is important to Trust the Process.

Stories of My Generation

By GUY TAL (Torrey, Utah) 27 August 2012

It feels, sometimes, as though invisible winds carry ideas and realizations among people of like minds. Telling my stories is the driving force behind my work. It is the reason I do what I do and live as I do and, I suppose, think as I do. Beyond merely recounting random events, the desire to share stories of my own experiences is also what drives me to seek such experiences, many of which end up transforming me in profound ways far beyond the images inspired by them.

It seems I am not alone. Recently I had the pleasure of presenting at a photography event, where I shared some of my stories and the way they guided my life. The previous day I sat through an excellent presentation by a younger photographer. He, too, talked about his stories and the telling of stories through images. I was encouraged by the fact that, like me, people of a younger generation also could appreciate many of the joys of living as a creative wanderer in a world where many may never experience life as I have. Talkin' 'bout my generation.

I like to imagine the life experiences of other people. I do so often when visiting ancient dwellings and cultural sites. I try to imagine the daily routines of those who built and occupied them; what it was like to be a child growing up there, what the proverbial "day in the life" was, and how these people responded to the natural beauty of the place, in a world without industry and electronics and motorized vehicles. I try not to romanticize too much. Modern life, I'm sure, is much easier in many ways than it was even decades ago. Still, it would be arrogant to assume that such lives—quieter, closer to the land, likely more spiritual and full of myth and wonder—were not, at least in some ways, better than ours.

I also imagine others' lives when encountering fellow travelers on the road: the woman and dog sleeping in the back of an old sedan in a remote rest stop on a freezing winter night in rural Nevada; the bleary-eyed young couple eating an early breakfast at a roadside diner, their U-Haul parked outside, en route to new places and new possibilities and new lives; the blonde in a convertible yellow Volkswagen zooming around the curves of a remote mountain road; or the hitchhiker in the middle of the desert, likely not aware of a sign a couple of hundred yards away warning motorists not to pick up hitchhikers due to the proximity of a jail. I have dozens of them carved into my memory. What I don't know, I try to guess and fill in.

Of course, there are also the solitary experiences — stories of wildness and wilderness: a face-off with a bighorn ram in a narrow canyon, the surreal shimmering of deserts in the summer heat, the bewitching scents of sagebrush and wet earth after a first rain, mountain meadows in bloom, glowing aspen groves on a perfectly silent and chilly autumn morning, arriving at a prom-

 . . . the woman and dog sleeping in the back of an old sedan in a remote rest stop on a freezing winter night in rural Nevada; . . .

inent summit after a long scramble as the last light of the day is fading and the world is bathed in purple and lavender, the crackle of campfires and the gurgle of streams and the whisper of breeze in forest canopies, and so many more.

I think of people who lived in the old house I now occupy and how different their lives were from mine. I think of the experiences of my childhood, before color television and computers and cellular phones and the Internet; a life I'm sure is familiar to some readers but that many already living today may never again be able to experience; a life where one can find perfect silence, spend hours in a field or forest or desert with nothing and no one for company other than their own thoughts, the timeless landscape and its natural inhabitants; a life where most time was spent out of doors and most interactions occurred in person. These multi-dimensional and multi-sensory experiences now reduced to virtual worlds of sensory deprivation and mindless banter; often accompanied with apathy or even fear of wild places, of relying on one's own faculties to partake in the things that make life itself possible – the things we evolved to find beautiful and meaningful, yet opted to give up in exchange for material comforts.

And I worry. Before my eyes I see the things that made my own life so rewarding rapidly disappearing, replaced with ever more confined spaces, ever more controlled environments, ever more generic and predictable lives, and ever fewer possibilities for mystery and discovery and thrill. I worry not just about the kind of world we leave for our children, but also about the kind of children we leave for our world.

I consider myself fortunate to have the freedom to venture into places where humans may never have been, where discoveries still await. I appreciate being able to grow some of my own food, and to wake up to silent mornings interrupted only by the chirping of birds, and to see a plethora of celestial lights on a dark night, free of light pollution. The day is not far when lives such as mine may be considered as primitive as those of cave dwellers;

 I consider myself fortunate to have the freedom to venture into places where humans may never have been, where discoveries still await.

yet I am sure cave life offered profoundly moving experiences, too, that are no longer possible.

There will soon be a time when we will be looked upon with disdain for having used potable water to wash and to adorn our dwellings with flowers just because they are beautiful. If futurists are to be believed, the next century will turn the vast majority of humans into transient resources for industry, crammed in tiny spaces in large cities centered on airports. Part of me, I regret to say, takes small comfort in mortality and in the knowledge that I will not have to live such a life.

Each society can point to the achievements and failures of its own generations. Here, in the United States, my predecessors—the baby boomers—brought with them economic prosperity in the wake of a great war, civil rights, the Vietnam war, television and Rock & Roll. According to a model put together by William Strauss and Neil Howe, the boomers were an idealist generation whereas mine—Generation X—is a reactive one. I fear, however, that our reaction will be remembered not as a positive one altogether. We instigated the personal computer revolution and brought the Internet to the public; we saw the end of the Cold War; we also brought consumerism and greed to levels never before seen in human history. We are the generation who learned about the evils of pollution, the risks of climate change, the dissonance of a growth-based economy, and the rise of global financial powers "too big to fail." We may well be remembered for being the last generation who still knew life before gadgetry, who saw the changing tides and could still do something about it ... but didn't.

Tell your stories with passion and eloquence. Keep alive in them the things and experiences and revelations that may not survive otherwise. Of the legacies we leave, very few may ultimately be more important than letting those who will follow know what life was like before the era of cramped confinement and social media. Tell stories of the thrill of experiencing the world in person, off line, and away from the cacophony of cities. Make your readers realize that growth is not the same as prosperity, that riches come in forms not always measurable in money, and that there is more magic in real reality than in any artifice of human conception.

Guy Tal (guytal.com) is a professional landscape and nature photographer, writer, author, blogger, teacher and wilderness guide.

PART 3: THE LOVE OF FAMILY

"The love of family and the admiration of friends is much more important than wealth and privilege." - Charles Kuralt

Saying Yes to Whatever the Future Holds

By BECKY ROBINSON (SE Michigan, NW Ohio) 24 November 2011

It's bedtime. The girls are asking for a story.

My repertoire of stories is limited. I've told them all lots of times, they want new ones, and I can't think of any.

Tell us a story about you and Daddy, they say.

Okay, I say: Have I told you about how Daddy asked me to marry him twice?

Tell us! they say, and I lean back against the white rails of the bottom bunk and tell the stories.

Oxford, Ohio. 1991.

The end of my sophomore year in college. I'm with a group of friends uptown on a Saturday evening. My boyfriend at the time, I'm not sure where he is.

It might be finals week. He might be studying. I don't remember.

There are four of us around the table, eating frozen yogurt from Styrofoam cups with long plastic spoons. Mine's chocolate.

The lone male in the group takes off a ring from his right hand. It's shaped like a wedding band but it has a colorful design. He bought the ring last summer while traveling in Turkey. He and his friend Vince each bought a ring to show their commitment to return to Turkey someday.

He holds up the ring, places it on the table; he asks: "Who wants to marry me and go to Turkey?"

I forget about my boyfriend for a moment (where is he? I can't remember) and I pick up the ring without hesitating. I slide it on my finger. I hold out my hand to admire the ring.

"I'll marry you and go to Turkey," I say.

I smile. Then I hand the ring back across the table. But I'm still thinking about the proposal.

I'm entranced by the possibility of going to Turkey and I'm intrigued by the guy across the table.

Kansas City, Missouri, August 1992.

I've just returned from a summer in Turkey. My face is tan and freckled from days in the sun and my hair is red from henna. I am in my parents' kitchen with...

With Daddy, right?

Yes, with Daddy. But he's not your Daddy yet.

I made him some peach cobbler. I serve him some cobbler and I sit down beside him. He grabs my hand.

I look down, close my eyes, thinking we're going to pray.

I feel him press something sharp into my palm. "What are you doing?" I say.

I look at him and he asks, "Will you marry me?" Then I let him slide the ring on my finger.

"Of course, I'll marry you," I say. And then we kiss. For the very first time.

(I embellish this part for the girls, while they're still young. I'm not ready for them to like boys or think about kissing. I'd like them to believe, for as long as possible, that kissing is what married people do. Or engaged people. Or whatever.

I also know, as I write it, that it will seem strange to you. I know it's unusual that we waited to kiss until our engagement. But we did, and it's part of the story.)

So, we kiss. And then, overcome by nerves or emotions, I run to the bathroom: heaving, sick. (Not a pretty part of the story, but also true.)

April, 2011

We celebrate 18 years of marriage. I said yes to two proposals and I am still saying yes, every day.

Yes: to the intriguing guy across the table.

Yes: to love. Yes: to this life we are sharing. Yes: to whatever the future holds.

Becky Robinson is a social media strategist, author and founder of *weavinginfluence.com* leading a team of more than 20 skilled professionals partnering with authors and thought leaders to grow their online influence and market their books. She formed Team Buzz Builder, a supportive community of bloggers that she mobilizes on behalf of authors. She also has an extensive network of online followers through the Twitter accounts @beckyrbnsn, @weaveinfluence, @teambuzzbuilder, and @teamfaithbuildr. Becky is the author of 12 Minutes to Change Your Day, Your Book Deserves a Celebration, and 31 Days of Twitter Tips: Grow Your Online Influence, 12 Minutes at a Time. She is a wife and mother of three daughters.

I'm Molly McClelland, Jeffrey's Mom

By MOLLY MCCLELLAND (Pittsburgh, Pennsylvania) 21 June 2011

In this my first entry for A Hopeful Sign, I find it most important to give you, my new readers, a framework for understanding me at present. It is now in my 34th year, that I have taken turbulent flight on a bold, new adventure called motherhood. As a new mother to Jeffrey John II (born December 21, 2010) and as a committed partner to Jeff, I am so grateful to be nurturing our new family in the best way we can, and on our own terms. It is through my two Jeff's that I know what life and love are all about.

It is also important that you know that I am a woman who has promised to remain true to all that she dreamed to do in her own right, and I will.

This is where I stand.

It only makes sense that this challenging balancing act has seen its fair share of instability. (I want you to think Leaning Tower of Pisa.) Recent ankle surgery has left me, champion of independence and self-sufficiency, asking for help and bringing a baby along for the ride. I'm sure this is a two-for-one deal that leaves A LOT to be desired.

(I'll admit to daily, personal struggles with common sense, good sense, practicality, and logistics. I can't imagine that it has been a joy for those I've dragged into this vortex. I know my life requires a whole lot of duct tape. I'm so sorry.)

My greatest lesson learned while on injured reserve: Humility is at once a Godsend and a bitter little pill to swallow. I am both awestruck by the love and support that surrounds me from family and from friends, and ready to bang my head off the wall for my dependence on others for nearly everything. Did I mention that the cast is on my right ankle? No driving.

On a positive, I have been able to use this time to get myself

 Parenting was not going to be perfect, seamless, or smooth.

prepared and focused on how I will define myself and the gift of life I have been given. In that all of my life's great journeys have begun with a single, completely unrelated step, I decided to organize the 500-plus pictures of Jeffrey's first months of life trapped, on my computer, camera, and phone.

Do you think it's too late to send a birth announcement? I should be ashamed.

This "little" project, which occupied all morning and half of the afternoon, provided a most mind-blowing stroll down memory lane. To see our lives in print, to see us change in such a divine way in the course of just five and a half months is nothing short of miraculous.

I had to laugh at our first pictures. We didn't have a clue. It was entirely appropriate for Jeff's zipper to be down in our first family photo. Parenting was not going to be perfect, seamless, or smooth.

Still the hospital saw us fit to take our sweet Jeffrey home, even though I hadn't cleaned behind the stove prior to his birth. (No one even swung by to check.) The knowledgeable hospital staff seemed fully confident that we could handle being parents; if only our faces revealed similar confidence. We were so afraid.

When I compared those first moments to our recent photos, I was struck by how the growth of our son served as a reminder of how far Jeff and I have come. We, too, have grown so much.

I also couldn't help but think about our future as a family. As parents and as people, there are just so many unknowns. There are so many questions: What challenges will we face? How will we respond? What kind of parents will we be? Will we raise a good, honest man? What will he take from us as his foundation? What will he decide to leave behind?

So many questions. This is where I stand.

It is an honor to share with you, my readers, my life and my learning curve.

Molly McClelland (momsaidwhat.com) is a writer, humorist, working mother, and the creator of a new blog called momsaidwhat. As a first-time, new mom to Jeffrey John II, Molly is using the power of words and laughter to help find a balance between her family and her ambition. Fingers crossed.

How Mama Got Her Happy Groove Back

By TARA RUMMELL BERSON (Middletown, New Jersey) 26 June 2011

crank•y [krang-kee]–adjective, crank•i•er, crank•i•est. 1. ill-tempered; grouchy; cross: I'm always cranky when I don't get enough sleep.

Yep, this definition pretty much sums up how I was feeling most of the time: Cross, grouchy, and in a semi-permanent state of aggravation. I grappled with these negative feelings, especially since I'm usually the person who people turn to when they need a pick-me-up! Always a people-pleaser, I didn't want to let my friends down, so I became a somewhat "closeted grump" — meaning that I'd still smile brightly and say, "I'm doing great!" when others asked me how I was doing, but on the inside I felt uninspired, blah, and to be honest, kind of bitchy!

As a mom of two kids under 5, I was growing more and more exhausted by my overwhelming to-do list and the constant multitasking yet lack of productivity. I was trying to be the perfect stay-at-home mother, while also freelance writing from home, which meant that I was usually up to the wee hours of the night trying to finish assignments. The lack of sleep made me irritable, and I also felt bummed out that my career wasn't going the way I'd hoped. Then I'd feel guilty for fretting about my professional status instead of being appreciative that I could stay at home with my kids, and the vicious crankiness cycle continued.

Luckily, something happened one Saturday morning in March (a few years ago) that made me view life from a healthier perspective. I was driving my 4 ½-year-old to swim lessons, and as we crossed over the bridge into the next town, I pointed out how pretty the river looked with the sun reflecting off of it. My son agreed, but said that he likes it more when the sun sets "because it's orange." When I told my husband about our exchange, he replied, "Who doesn't appreciate a good sunset?" And as I sipped my coffee, their combined comments got me thinking about happiness, and how refreshingly easy it is to feel a moment of joy when you look at or think about something you like. The key is to appreciate it while it's happening and to embrace those feelings of hope and optimism, as well as the contentment it brings.

I used to write a monthly column for a national women's magazine called "Time for You," and on that page I'd list 5 things to be happy about. While it was sometimes challenging to come up with these cheery little nuggets, I always smiled while reviewing the final list each month. With that in mind, I decided to start a blog called The Crankiness Crusher ™ that would encourage me to feel the same way. I desperately needed to learn how to zero in on the good in each day so that I could start chipping away at my alter ego (who I comically refer to as the evil Dr. Crankenstein). As often as I could, I'd write about something specific that crushed my crankiness that day. These 'Crankiness Crushers' were something as simple as enjoying a few moments of solitude with my grande skinny caramel macchiato or a random occurrence like appearing on "The Dr. Oz Show" – which was pretty cool, by the way! Chronicling these experiences has been cathartic. As a writer, it satisfied my need to get things down. I've been able to reveal the rawest parts of myself and take my crankiness out of the closet. Hopefully, I'm helping others learn how to channel their own negativity in a healthier manner.

The focus of The Crankiness Crusher ™ is not so much about maintaining a constant good mood, but more about remembering to look for and appreciate the happy in each day – even if it's something small like a freshly-mowed lawn, your favorite summer song on the radio, or eating an ice cream cone with your family. When you're encouraged to find at least one good thing that happens daily, that positive thought can make you feel saner, more balanced, and less blah.

Throughout my anti-crankiness journey, I've realized that when you're not über crabby, it's much easier to deal with minor annoyances and issues. It's also made me feel more generous, forgiving, and compassionate. As a mom, I've had more energy and the emotional balance to tackle things that would normally set me off (like the perpetual whininess in my household!). The truth is, when you're happy, you're empowered to be a better person. And who doesn't strive for that?

Tara Rummell Berson (crankinesscrusher.com) *is an associate producer for KnowMore.tv, a health & wellness website, an adjunct communications/ media professor, and the founder of The Crankiness Crusher ™. She lives in Middletown, NJ with her husband, two kids, and dog. Not surprisingly, she's always looking to find simple ways to be happy/grateful/not cranky on a daily basis.*

The Bar Mitzvah Boy

By AIMEE LEDEWITZ WEINSTEIN (Tokyo, Japan) 17 September 2012

I didn't know that poised, confident young man who stood before the congregation leading the service. He bore a strong resemblance to my 13-year-old son, but surely my child wasn't as talented and engaging as this boy — or was he?

Strangely enough it was indeed my child up there. Bailey, age thirteen, recently celebrated his bar mitzvah. Literally translated, it means "son of the commandments" and it's the Jewish coming-of-age ceremony that recognizes a boy's entrance into adulthood in the eyes of world Jewry. It generally involves leading a service and reading from the Torah, all in Hebrew. So this is something for which Bailey had been studying for months.

The unusual part of Bailey's bar mitzvah, however, is that he is doing it twice. The first one was in August in the U.S. with our entire family, and the second one is in October with our Tokyo community. It was important to Bailey to have this celebration with his extended family, all of whom are in the U.S., but also with his own friends, at his own synagogue, with the rabbi who had been teaching him for the past three years, even though that place was halfway across the globe. So while I kept on him to study, he was largely self-motivated, wanting to please his grandparents in the U.S. and his beloved rabbi in Tokyo, even if that meant learning two different services.

One of the beauties of Judaism is that the readings from the Torah are cyclical and proscribed. I feel very comfortable knowing that every Jew around the world is reading the same section of the Torah on any given Saturday. But given that parameter, it meant that Bailey would have to learn a different portion for the October bar mitzvah than the August one. And still, he never batted an eyelash.

On this special day, Bailey carried with him, on his person, proof of his heritage. He was wearing my grandfather's mezuzah, a casing containing a special prayer, around his neck; he wore my other grandfather's watch. He wore my husband's grandfather's tie-tack, and as the icing on the cake, he wore his grandfather's tallis, or prayer shawl, which his grandfather's grandfather had worn to his bar mitzvah. Bailey had a piece of ceremonial regalia from his great-great-grandfather.

Only moments before starting the service, Bailey had dragged me away from the gathering crowd to a private room where no

 When he was through, he stood up and looked straight at me. He looked so dapper, that boy of mine.

one could see us. "I can't do it," he said, and started to cry. My first reaction, which thankfully I didn't show, was panic. Luckily rationality took over and I just held him and let him cry for a moment. Any mother would tell you that sometimes all a kid needs is a good hug, not words or even treats. Just a hug. "It's a lot of pressure," I told him, hoping to validate his feelings. "Do you want to do a quick run-through right this second?"

Bailey nodded and dried his eyes while I snuck out and retrieved his study materials. We had a quick, ten-minute, last-second rehearsal right there. When he was through, he stood up and looked straight at me. He looked so dapper, that boy of mine. He wore his first full-on suit, a blue striped shirt and a snazzy tie. The shoes, straight from Nordstrom's, tied the whole outfit together.

I searched his eyes as he looked at me. "You're okay," I said to him and he nodded. I repeated it. "You are okay."

This boy, this baby of my heart, as I used to call him when he was little, stood up in front of 120 of our closest friends and family members and performed like a champ. No one would know that he had had a little meltdown only moments prior. He sang with a rich, strong tone and spoke clearly without a waver to his voice. He delivered his d'var Torah, a word of Torah that explained what he read and his interpretations of it, without missing a beat. He bantered lightly with the rabbi, and hugged his grandparents when they went up to share the sweet moment with him.

At times like these, it's hard to recognize the sometimes-surly child who makes an appearance at the breakfast table each morning, or the scatterbrained kid who can never find all of the elements of a homework assignment at one time. But it is moments like these that give us hope. It is moments like these that connect us to the past, yet I could see a glimpse of the man my son has the potential to become. In an increasingly cynical world where religion sometimes takes a backseat to other, more modern activities, watching a child take his place next to his ancestors as a young man proud of his heritage and ready to take on all of the rights and responsibilities thereof, is like receiving a gift of a vision of the future.

After the service, there was dinner and dancing, and Bailey danced. He danced in Florida and he danced in Tokyo a few months later. Joy, hope and pride all mixed together to form a twinkle in his eye and he whirled and played. I have a feeling that I will recognize that twinkle many times in the years to come. I cannot wait to watch.

Dr. Aimee Weinstein (TokyoWriter.com) is a writer and writing professor who has lived eight out of the last ten years in Tokyo, Japan. She received her doctorate from the Department of Higher Education at George Mason University and has held positions at Temple University Japan, The George Washington University, and George Mason University. She has taught a variety of writing courses, from freshman composition to advanced expository writing. Her work has been published in Kaleidescope, Tokyo Weekender, inTouch, and Asian Jewish Life. She also maintains a regular blog where she fondly observes Tokyo life through the eyes of an American expat and writes about writing. Aimee currently resides in Tokyo with her supportive husband and two beautiful children, where she continues to write and help others in their writing.

Regret is Dead Weight

By KAREN VELEZ (Sacramento, California) 24 August 2012

A friend of mine had a baby not too long ago. That baby is about four months old now. My friend shares stories and photos and her excitement at being a new mama. She is so full of innocence and love. Who could blame her? Her baby is beautiful.

A little over a week ago, she shared a short video of the baby interacting with her. She would say something. The baby would move his arms and legs like he was dancing, look at her, smile, and "goo-goo" and babble back when she stopped talking. The cadence of their banter is unmistakable. That baby babbles with meaning. With purpose. I can see that words are just around the corner.

She blows raspberries on his tummy. He laughs. He coos.

So that is what I was missing.

Yes, six years later, in a short video clip, I saw, for the first time in my life, how another kind of baby interacts with his mama. Ouch.

I didn't see it with my own son.

I was blindsided.

That baby is adorable, and watching that baby and his mama cut me deeply. Obviously, that was not her intent. I loved seeing the video. I had joy in the moment, knowing the sheer innocence and loving bond it represented. And then I cried, silently, alone.

At the time of my own son's birth, I had never cared for an infant. I never babysat a child. I never had a sibling. No nephews, nieces, friends with children. Nada. I did not know that the child in my arms 24/7 was different. I did not know we were missing milestones like I saw last week.

The interaction without words.

The mutual expressions of love.

I saw instant "reactions" during an exchange filled with love.

And I felt happy and sad, excitement and regret. Regret that I was blind to see my own child was different earlier. But what would have changed? Would I have pursued a year or two of ABA (Applied Behavioural Analysis)? How would I have found ABA then (for my autistic child)? Would I have found the people who have given my son so much? They were not even located in our region then. Would I have searched as deeply? Would I have written about it? I don't know. Would things be better, different, worse?

Regret and conjecture serves no purpose other than to beget sadness and doubt.

I pulled out an old baby album. I cannot find any videos of him. At all. Is that strange?

I looked through photographs. In the hundreds of pictures I took of my baby, most were of him sleeping. Maybe because he looked so peaceful and I felt those moments were so rare. In all

 Regret and conjecture serves no purpose other than to beget sadness and doubt.

those pictures, so few were with his eyes open. In most of those, he looks dazed, surprised or confused. There were only five I found where he was smiling.

Three were with his daddy. Two were alone. None were with me.

I don't think I am bitter. Sad is more like it. But since that serves no purpose, I have to let go.

The beauty of those moments, the smiles there are captured for eternity. There is a deep love between the boys in my life.

And for me, I feel the deepest, most fulfilling love of my life in my love for my son. I feel enormous joy from his beautiful smile outside to the innocence of the inner core of his being. I love all of him as he is, now and forever.

He's grown.

He says, "I love you, mommy," every day.

And I relish every syllable. Because each one is a gift. I understand that.

Regret is dead weight. Gratitude lifts me up and brings me into the light. In that light, I know how much I have to be grateful for. I am lucky to be mother to the little boy I call my own.

> **Karen Velez (solodialogue.wordpress.com)** *is a lawyer and the mom of a 7 year old boy with autism. She works part time and spends the rest driving here and there and everywhere for her son's various therapies. Instead of trying cases, she now plays Pac-man and watches SpongeBob. She wears old sweaters and jeans and always, always flat shoes to run after my son. Yeah, it's different but she wouldn't change it for anything. The love of her child is the most powerful, beautiful and rewarding aspect of her life.*

No Longer "New" Mom

By MOLLY MCCLELLAND (Pittsburgh, Pennsylvania) 13 Dec 2011

Jeffrey turns one in just over a week. I'm thinking it's time to drop the "New" from my "Mom" title. I'm not a "New Mom" anymore. Just Mom.

I like that.

For me, this year is a total contradiction. It is hard to believe that a year has passed so quickly; and at the same time life has been wonderfully slow and full of milestones, as witnessed through the growth and change in our infinitely happy and healthy son. And while I thought that my post on Jeffrey's first year would reflect, recount, and revel in these milestones, I'd rather just say thank you to my son.

Jeffrey, you have made realize the most valuable lesson of all; that each moment of life is a gift of immeasurable worth and should be viewed in wonderment. Life, in and of its simple self, is joy.

Through watching Jeffrey's awakening to his world, I am reminded of how mind-blowing each moment can be. To watch him sift through and handful of grass, or inspect a leaf he's found on the ground, to squeeze mud through his fingers, or boldly wave a stick in the air; well, needless to say I've stopped to take closer notice of things myself.

He's right, they are unbelievable and awe-inspiring.

Jeffrey's one-year old spirit shakes the film and dust of grown-up-dom from my 35-year old soul, and forces the child out to play. Jeffrey shows me how important it is that I get off the wheel, get on the ground, get some dirt under my nails, and just have a bit of fun

(I've noticed, you don't typically see groups of adults engaged in play on the floor. Strangely, it's not been widely received in most social circles. It's unfortunate, really. I think Jeffrey is on to something. Maybe an occasional game of peek-a-boo at the office would take some of the nastiness out of things.)

With Jeffrey, nothing else matters but whatever moment is directly in front of him. He's not stuck in the trials and tribulations of what happened in the past; nor is he even for a second tied up in the thinking of what is yet to come.

Imagine that.

I thank Jeffrey for helping me to understand that there is nothing in life that I can accomplish, that will ever be as gratifying as the simple moments that make up this grand life. I owe it to him to keep this simple, childlike perspective present in my mind, no matter how complex the cold world of grownups can be.

In this year, I have been so regularly reminded of how fortunate my life has been, and I am infinitely grateful for all that I have. And while I look forward to all that Jeffrey's next year will bring to my life, I'll spend less time looking forward and more time in the dirt.

Molly McClelland (momsaidwhat.com) *is a writer, humorist, working mother, and the creator of a new blog called momsaidwhat. As a first-time, new mom to Jeffrey John II, Molly is using the power of words and laughter to help find a balance between her family and her ambition. Fingers crossed.*

Heading Out—Starting Them Young

By BRUCE MASTERMAN (High River, Alberta) 04 October 2011

It was a glorious fall afternoon, with the drab green foliage of trees and willows transformed into dazzling displays of yellows and red.

I often think that if seasons were people, autumn would be the wildly eccentric relative you love to visit. There's nothing subdued or boring about fall. Going strictly on looks, the other three seasons are relatively lackluster. Autumn's colours are vivid and varied, bursting from nature's palette in a remarkable celebration of brilliant contrasts.

It's simultaneously kaleidoscopic, psychedelic and magical. Autumn is my favourite season, no question.

But as I drove through the mountains west of the foothills town where we live, I was amazed by what I saw in the various cars and family vans that I met. Even though most of them held children, few kids were actually seeing Mother Nature's spectacular show.

Young faces were glued to movies playing on screens above them. Children were looking down, apparently reading or, more likely, playing with some kind of computer game, oblivious to the fall magic playing out around them. In surprisingly few vehicles, young passengers actually paid attention to the view outside. Even most adult passengers seemed to be otherwise occupied.

To me, the experience was just another symptom of an ever-growing malaise that threatens the future of our great outdoors: many children either aren't getting the chance to experience nature, or they don't know how to appreciate it even if they do venture out.

Recent studies have shown that increased urbanization, popularity of video games, growth of single parent families and a general disinterest all have contributed to a decline in the number of kids enjoying the outdoors.

In a cleverly perceptive—and more than slightly tongue-in-cheek—column in The New Yorker magazine last March, writer Ellis Weiner introduced readers to a new "astounding multipurpose activity platform" that he called GOING OUTSIDE, which he said would "revolutionize how you spend your time."

"GOING OUTSIDE is not a game or a program, not a device or an app, not a protocol or an operating system," Weiner wrote. "Instead, it's a comprehensive experiential mode that lets you perceive and do things firsthand, without any intervening media or technology."

Among its many benefits, Weiner points out GOING OUTSIDE enables "complete interactivity with inanimate objects, animals and Nature. Enjoy the texture of real grass, listen to authentic birds, or discover a flower that has grown up out of the earth. By GOING OUTSIDE you'll be astounded by the number and variety of things there are in the world."

Using modern computer language to highlight the benefits

 But as I drove through the mountains west of the foothills town where we live, I was amazed by what I saw in the various cars and family vans that I met.

of being outside is both enlightening and slightly disturbing. So many of us, adults and children alike, are finding ourselves increasingly engaged in a techno-land of pixels, downloads, instant messaging and apps for every occasion. But along the path to this online fantasy world we risk losing touch with what's very real and important in the natural world around us.

Many adults are willing to make that trade-off, but it behooves all of us to make sure children have every chance to be outdoors. And what if they don't, you might ask?

Well, for starters, they're being robbed of a chance to appreciate a world beyond classrooms, shopping malls, the Internet and other places where a natural sense of wonder seldom exists. By not having a chance to hike, fish, camp and develop a relationship with nature, they aren't discovering where they fit into the grand scheme of things, and how their actions can impact natural places and wild things. And without that level of stewardship awareness on the part of our future policy makers, how can we hold out much hope for what lies ahead?

Thankfully, there is hope. There is hope in the admittedly minority of dedicated adults—including many single parents I know—who still take kids outdoors, and in many organizations such as Guides, Cubs and Scouts, Junior Forest Wardens and various other groups that teach outdoor education through hands-on experiences. I've had the honour of being involved in several such organizations, including with our own two daughters, Chelsea and Sarah, when they were younger. But the foundation was laid well before they were old enough to belong to any group.

Starting when they needed to be carried in a pack or pulled on a sled while we skied, my wife Karen and I shared with them the

---

 People who are introduced to the outdoors as youngsters become its biggest allies later in life.

---

wonders of the outdoors. They learned to identify animals and birds but, more importantly, they learned to love seeing them in their natural habitat, and came to appreciate their respective places in the world.

At age two, they both started learning not only how to catch fish, but also about the different types, and the places where fish lived. Along the way they learned to respect the rules we had to follow and understand why we didn't litter or harm their environment. Through fishing they also learned a lot about themselves.

On Sarah's birthday one spring we took several young girls on a nature scavenger hunt. We walked a mountain trail while they busied themselves finding paper and other litter, pine cones, wildflowers and other prizes. Garbage was the only prize they were allowed to pick. They had fun watching squirrels and birds, and competing to see who could collect the most litter.

We camped with them from when they were very young, and picnicked in all four seasons. We cross-country skied and hiked. We frequented places where they saw wildlife such as deer, elk, moose and bears. We made a game of spotting animals from the car, with a nebulous prize (a candy bar or maybe a hug?) going to the child who saw the first deer, or coyote, or whatever.

They both developed not just an appreciation of nature, but a love for it that remains strong today even as they're well into their 20's. When they both moved to a major West Coast city, they insisted on packing their fly-fishing gear. Karen told me a few minutes ago that Sarah planned to go canoeing with a friend today.

People who are introduced to the outdoors as youngsters become its biggest allies later in life. And with nature under constant siege, it needs all the friends it can get.

Bruce Masterman (brucemasterman.com) is an award-winning Alberta writer, book author, photographer, magazine assignment editor and college journalism instructor with a passion for conservation and almost anything outdoorsy. He contributes to various magazines, including Outdoor Canada, The Conservator, West, Reader's Digest and several others. Bruce is the author of two nonfiction books—Heading Out: A Celebration of the Great Outdoors in Calgary and Southern Alberta, and Paradise Preserved: The Ann and Sandy Cross Conservation Area—and has contributed to five others.

You Gotta Have Hope

By AIMEE LEDEWITZ WEINSTEIN (Tokyo, Japan) 24 July 2012

When I finished college, I got a plum job right in downtown New York City. Of course, being my first job out of school, the salary was next-to-nothing, and there was no way I could afford an apartment in Manhattan. My grandparents, like they always had throughout my life, came to my rescue. They lived in Teaneck, New Jersey, about four miles over the George Washington Bridge, and an easy New Jersey Transit ride to the Port Authority Bus Terminal in Midtown every day. Thus I became a commuter and resident of my grandparents' house for two years.

When I think back on that time what sticks out most to me is not the fun—and occasional monotony—of reading the New York Times on the bus, or the beautiful streets of Manhattan at Christmas, or even the job that I didn't like all that much, but the atmosphere created by two people who never expected to have a child come home to live again. They were never ones to sit around, my grandparents. Right up until the last year of his life when he was 82, my grandfather worked as a pharmacist at the Veteran's Hospital in the Bronx. Three days a week my grandmother drove him into the city at 8am, and then went back to pick him up at 5pm. He never used public transportation, and they never bought a second car. This was their ritual and it worked for them. They had other quirky habits involving who showered first and who ate breakfast first, and who watered the plants versus who washed the dishes, and other such things that made sense only to them. What I didn't know at the time was that they were teaching me through example about the true language of love and

---

 They had other quirky habits involving who showered first and who ate breakfast first, . . .

---

the commitment and practice of a long, enduring marriage.

Dinner time was my favorite though. I didn't get home from work until after 6:30pm every day, but they always waited for me to eat. It was common for the three of us to spend more than ninety minutes at the table, eating, talking, and going over the events of the day. At the time, they were working on computerizing Papa's pharmacy, and my grandfather was fascinated with the process of entering the patient information and how the machine could "remember" each person, their medications, and other such information. He had been a pharmacist on a hospital ship in WWII, so this process and progress delighted him.

Grandma was a good cook. Her holiday dinners were feasts of the eyes and palates, and never-ending to boot. On a day-to-day basis, however, she was much more controlled. In a very civilized way, we started each meal with half a grapefruit in the winter and a slice of melon in the summer. Always health and diet conscious and ahead of her time, she plated our dinners for us. If you think about a plate as a clock, she put the protein from three to six, the starch from six to nine and then the rest, from nine to three, was vegetables. While the women in the family watched their weight religiously, there wasn't an ounce of extra fat on my grandfather.

For the first few weeks of my sojourn in their home, one ritual in particular caught my eye. Every night as she plated the dinner, she spooned the vegetables out of the pot and right on to the dishes, which already held the meat and starch. Every night, my grandfather asked the same question: "Why don't you use a slotted spoon? I don't like so much water from the pot on my plate."

Every night my grandmother had the same response: "I don't have a slotted spoon."

And that's where they left it.

Finally, after about a month, I watched the exchange for the thirtieth time and I had to say something. "Papa," I asked, "Why don't you go out and buy Grandma a slotted spoon?"

"Aimee," he said with that funny little twinkle that he always

---

 Every night my grandmother had the same response: "I don't have a slotted spoon."

---

had in his eye, "You gotta have hope."

At the time, my grandmother and I both laughed at him, and then the three of us laughed together and went on with our meal. But now, nearly twenty years later, the little exchange still sticks with me.

He didn't care about the slotted spoon. He cared about her. She plated his dinner every night with those vegetables because she cared about him. Their banter was their own private language they used to show that love. And the whole "hope" thing, well, that was my grandfather's personality. He looked forward to the wonderment of the computers and all sorts of other things he couldn't have imagined when he was a young man. Hope is what helped the two of them survive the depression, the war, raising their family, their extensive travels, and then the quieter time together in their later years.

My grandmother is still living, still my very best friend, and she says now that I idealize him too much sometimes, but I disagree. I know he was a human and had faults like everyone else. I guess

I was just impressionable at that time in my life and their lessons showed me something to which to aspire in my own long-term marriage, as my husband and I create our own languages of love and care that would be incomprehensible to the outside world. My husband and I hit obstacles, of course, but we have learned to use our language—not always verbal—to work through them. It's the definition of hope in action every day.

Oh, and I own a slotted spoon, too.

Dr. Aimee Weinstein (TokyoWriter.com) is a writer and writing professor who has lived eight out of the last ten years in Tokyo, Japan. She received her doctorate from the Department of Higher Education at George Mason University and has held positions at Temple University Japan, The George Washington University, and George Mason University. She has taught a variety of writing courses, from freshman composition to advanced expository writing. Her work has been published in Kaleidescope, Tokyo Weekender, inTouch, and Asian Jewish Life. She also maintains a regular blog where she fondly observes Tokyo life through the eyes of an American expat and writes about writing. Aimee currently resides in Tokyo with her supportive husband and two beautiful children, where she continues to write and help others in their writing.

Bibliophiles and Bookworms

By BECKY ROBINSON (SE Michigan, NW Ohio) 03 August 2011

A couple of weekends ago, my family and I spent some time at our favorite thrift store. We all love browsing for books.

I chose a stack of books two feet high—including Guy Kawasaki's Rules for Revolutionaries—for less than the price of one new book.

When I got home, I discovered that Kawasaki had autographed the book, using his signature at the time—"Kick Butt."

I often share books with others when I'm done, but I can't imagine ever passing along any of the books I've gotten recently from author friends: the ones they took time to personally sign for me.

When an author (especially one I know personally), takes time to autograph my book, it becomes more than a book; it's a keepsake.

The attachment I feel toward autographed books reminds me of an old tradition in my family.

My grandfather enjoyed giving books to which he would add a special inscription. In his familiar, loopy script, he would write, to the book's intended recipient, a note like this:

To Becky,

I could not have written this book without your wise guidance and insights.

With love,

And then he would sign the AUTHOR'S name.

This tradition held so tightly that even though my grandfather has been gone for nearly a decade, my siblings, my mom, or I will still occasionally do the same: include pretend and effusive autographs in the books we give to each other as gifts.

I imagine a friend of my mother's, unaware, borrowing a book and discovering that Julia Child credits my mother with her success. Or that Stephen King counts her among his close personal friends.

I picture my mom setting the record straight: "Oh, no, that was my father. Just a joke. I don't really know Julia Child."

This tradition, to me, is an indicator of what we value as a family.

We are bibliophiles and bookworms.

I think it would make my grandfather smile to see the collection of books on my shelf, truly signed by the authors. Or to see my photos from a conference this spring, when I met Ken Blanchard and Jim Kouzes. If he were alive, I would certainly ask those friends to inscribe a book for him:

To George,

Whose loving influence has made a difference in so many lives.

He could put it on a shelf with all his other "autographed" books.

Becky Robinson is a social media strategist, author and founder of **weavinginfluence.com** leading a team of more than 20 skilled professionals partnering with authors and thought leaders to grow their online influence and market their books. She formed Team Buzz Builder, a supportive community of bloggers that she mobilizes on behalf of authors. She also has an extensive network of online followers through the Twitter accounts @beckyrbnsn, @weaveinfluence, @teambuzzbuilder, and @teamfaithbuildr. Becky is the author of 12 Minutes to Change Your Day, Your Book Deserves a Celebration, and 31 Days of Twitter Tips: Grow Your Online Influence, 12 Minutes at a Time. She is a wife and mother of three daughters.

Lessons From My Son

By KAREN VELEZ (Sacramento, California) 03 July 2011

Every day the world goes by at a rapid pace. Out there, the world is filled with tragedy, anger, greed, lust and hate. Sometimes, it seeps in. Mostly though, I feel lucky that the world slows down and I find peace whenever I am with my son. Yes, I'm talking about my screaming-yelling-worrying-me-making-me-tear-my-hair-out son. He has taught me many valuable things.

When you have a child with autism, you change. Your priorities change. You acquire knowledge of neurological functioning than you could not care less about before. You value things differently. Here are a couple off the top of my head.

Patience

A child repeating a sentence over and over doesn't sound like much, does it? Maybe once or twice or over a couple of months. For me, it's gone on for minimum of two years. To understand a little bit about this, just ask someone to read this paragraph below over and over and over again with heightened inflection, and variation in tone and volume:

"*The truck is purple. The truck is purple. The truck is purple. Mommy, the truck is purple. What color is the truck? What color is the truck? The truck is purple. Do you know the color of the truck? The truck is purple."*

From this simple example, I can tell you I have learned patience. Repetition is not that bad. After a while, it's almost part of the background noise. Yes, it is annoying most of the time, but I've learned that my son is processing language, meaning, and sometimes searching for words to assign to the thoughts he wishes to convey. My impatience and annoyance is insignificant compared to the processes the little guy is undergoing to communicate with me.

Along the same line, with this simple repetition, I have learned that people learn in different ways. I've never taken any courses in education or teaching. I've come to have a deep appreciation for the many teachers in my son's life whether they are labeled therapists or teachers. Because my son absorbs his environment and communicates differently from neurotypical children, teaching involves different methods and systems. Those systems are proven. I've seen the improvements. Sharing knowledge is a complicated and rewarding process.

Gratitude
Along the lines of those who provide my son with daily and weekly assistance, I have more gratitude than I can verbally express. It actually pours from my very being because I am so grateful and appreciative that each of these patient individuals works with my son.

Strength, Determination & Persistence
With his education, my son has amazing strengths. He has been able to read since he was about 2.5 years old. He can spell words by sound. He reads enough to manipulate an iPad with ease and navigate through a video game without anyone showing him how. Yet, he struggles holding a writing implement and making any type of legible letters, numbers or pictures.

Despite his utter dislike for writing implements of any sort, he sits and struggles on a daily basis in writing. Transferring the letters he reads through his head, through his muscles into his hand and onto paper is a huge struggle. He tries. Ever so slowly, he is making some legible print.

Sometimes, he will have an overwhelmingly strong desire to tell me something but the words will come out wrong. I won't understand. He will start again. I can see, through his facial expressions that he is painfully searching to give me the words. I wait. He persists. Sometimes he gets it out. Sometimes he does not. He does not give up. He does not get down. Sometimes he will get frustrated but he will re-boot and start again. Without any complaints. He just does it.

Innocence & Simplicity

My son has a lot of toys. No, really. A lot. Despite that fact, he will find joy in the simplest of objects. He will spend the entirety of his bath with a plastic cup, filling it up and dumping out the water. This is a favorite bath time activity. Give him a blanket and he will crawl underneath and call it a fort. Give him a small bottle of bubbles and you will see some of the biggest smiles and laughter you've ever seen. Give him a rock and he will examine it, bang it on the ground, roll it, throw it and laugh. Simplicity.

Each of these acts is born of innocent curiosity. He can find amusement with the most mundane of objects because of the purity and innocence of young life and the natural curiosity of the young, scientific mind.

At this age, he is actually excessively polite at times. "I want to read," he says to me while sitting at the table while I write. "You can read anything you want to," I respond. He is off to his bookshelf where he sits and reads quietly.

This is some of the most precious time I spend just watching him read or pour water from a cup, seeing him smile and laugh at bubbles.

And of course, all these lessons lead very naturally to enhancing the love I feel for him. I am a lucky mommy and this is just a small sample of the many lessons my son has taught me.

Karen Velez (solodialogue.wordpress.com) *is a lawyer and the mom of a 7 year old boy with autism. She works part time and spends the rest driving here and there and everywhere for her son's various therapies. Instead of trying cases, she now plays Pac-man and watches SpongeBob. She wears old sweaters and jeans and always, always flat shoes to run after my son. Yeah, it's different but she wouldn't change it for anything. The love of her child is the most powerful, beautiful and rewarding aspect of her life.*

The Secret to a Happy Marriage: A Pair of Rockers and Two Good Quilts!

By JOHN MCLAUGHLIN (Bathurst, New Brunswick) 25 October 2011

Our eldest daughter got married this fall on the same day that we celebrated our own 28th anniversary. This, of course, caused me to contemplate the many mysteries of a long and successful marriage, to formulate some kind of advice for this happy young couple about to embark on their own journey towards ever-after.

Rocking chairs, I decided. That's the secret. Two comfortable, durable rockers, and a couple of great, heavy quilts to go with them.

I am a happy man when I sit out on my front verandah, happier still when Cathy is rocking right beside me. She jokes about how we're going to sprout roots out there, and how the neighbours must wonder if we do anything else but rock away long moments, sometimes together, sometimes alone.

We once lived in an old townhouse on a great little downtown street in our small community, and we'd spend languid hours enjoying the space on our big old covered porch. That's where we first developed our love of rocking chairs. Deep into the fall, we'd swaddle ourselves in our old fashioned quilts, and we'd watch the neighborhood happen before us. It was like living on *Sesame Street*, I'd say, with the fireman, the grocer and the mailwoman all waving to us as they would go by. People would stop by on their way home from church, or while out walking their dogs, and we'd exchange pleasantries, or comment on the goings-on in the world around us.

We've dragged our rockers inside the house in the winter, and placed them before the fireplace. Our babies were cherished in rockers. Our dreams for them were imagined there. Our plans for our own happiness were nurtured there. When we designed our new home, which we built two years ago, we knew it all must begin with a sweeping front verandah, a space large enough for several rocking chairs, so our family and friends could rock along with us.

At the same time, a rocking chair can heighten the benefits of being alone with one's thoughts. I find a book is more likely to engulf me when I read it in my rocker. A stressful day is made easier when I kick the runners into high gear, and I allow balanced perspective to settle over me as I sort out solutions to problems, or just release pent up tension.

Our gift to the newlyweds, then, was the most sensible of all. We bought them a pair of good rockers and two really great quilts. May they find happiness rocking together, side by side, imagining their own possibilities.

John McLaughlin is Deputy Minister at the New Brunswick Department of Education & Early Childhood Development. As a former teacher and superintendent of schools, he believes the highest goal of education should be to nurture in students a sense of goodness, so they graduate from high school equipped not just with strong academic skills, but also a desire to contribute positively to the world, and to care for its people. John and his wife, Cathy, have four grown daughters, and they live in Bathurst on New Brunswick's beautiful northeastern coast.

Reinventing Mama

By AIMEE LEDEWITZ WEINSTEIN (Tokyo, Japan) 06 March 2012

For twelve years, my life has revolved around kids and kid activities. Even though I have usually worked at least part time, my first priority has always been the munchkins. I've been involved with their schools, done charity work with them, had dinner with them almost every night and fretted over every whim and trifle that has come into their lives. However, a little while ago, I had a glimpse into my future—my kid-free future.

That particular week my daughter's school had a few days off for a mid-winter holiday, or as it's commonly called, a ski break. I couldn't get the days off from teaching, so I sent her with a good family friend on a community ski trip. My son was headed to the Valentine's Day dance on Friday night. On Thursday, we got word that since the flu was so rampant in his school, they were cancelling the dance—too many pre-teens in close proximity to each other. Of course my son was upset, but only for a minute because he and his friend cooked up the idea of a double date to the movies. The dance was not happening and I couldn't think of a good reason why the group "date" thing wasn't a good substitute. It was one of those parenting moments when it took all of my self-control not to shout, "I'm not ready!"

My husband had spent the balance of this winter working at a client site out of the country, so he wasn't in town at the time. It was left to me to handle this date thing. I got home from work at 5pm, and Bailey had to leave for the movies at about 5:30. He had had a snack and planned to eat something at the theater. He had some money in his pocket and was prepared to spend it on his own movie ticket as well as the girl's.

A second or two after I got into the house, Bailey said, "Mom, Star Trek is on. Can we sit on the couch for a few minutes to watch?"

Certainly I wasn't going to refuse. He actually sat right next to me on the couch, his legs touching mine. Bailey is a snuggly kind of kid (don't tell him I told you) and he leaned right up against me slouching a little so his head was on my shoulder. I didn't dare move a muscle; I just squeezed his leg. I sat there with my son staring at the meaningless flickering images before me, going through all the moments in the past that led us here, to this day, to this moment. The baby of my heart, as I had called him all his life, was becoming the young man I knew he could be, and he still stopped to put his head on his mother's shoulder.

After about fifteen minutes, he jumped up suddenly, proclaiming that he really had to go if he wanted to be there on time.

I jumped into action with him, making sure he had his phone and his wallet in his pocket, and reminding him to come right home after the movie. Tokyo is an amazing city. Without a moment's hesitation I could let my twelve-year-old son head out to the movies on his own and wait for him to come back without worrying about his safety. He promised, kissed me, and threw a

 I sat there with my son staring at the meaningless flickering images before me, going through all the moments in the past that led us here, to this day, to this moment.

vague "love you" over his shoulder in my general direction before zipping off down the street.

And I went back inside the house from my perch on the front stoop. I shut the door. I stood there staring at it for a second, and then, without warning, I sat down hard on the floor and burst into tears.

My husband was away on business, my daughter was up skiing, and my son had gone out on a movie date. It was Friday night and I was home alone with nothing to do.

That's what I mean about seeing into my future: the kids were busy and I would have to think up something to do all on my own. There was no one to whom I was responsible for the next three plus hours and my time was my own to fill however I liked.

At first the idea of that much time alone felt scary. I missed my babies. I missed the running after them, the picking up after them, and even, in a weak moment, bathing them. I couldn't help but think of the past few years of nightly homework patrol and activity shuffle. All of that was eventually going to come to an end and for the first time I could picture that alternate reality. Those two amazing kids would probably become amazing adults with whom I'd hopefully have a great relationship, but at some point, they would be on their own and I would have a different life.

It took me a few minutes to pick myself up off the floor. It was cold down there, though, and the kitchen would be warmer. Then I realized that I could eat the leftovers from the night before all by myself. In fact, I could make popcorn and eat the whole bag. Perhaps I could even put on a chick flick and stretch out on the long sofa that I was all mine for a few hours. Wait a minute! This wasn't going to be all bad after all! A long time ago, a friend once told me that the purpose of an education is so that you're never bored. I am almost never bored and I wouldn't be bored or feel sorry for myself this night either.

When Bailey came home around 9:30, he found me watching

Before that night, I never thought about the changes in me in response to the growth of the children.

the end of an episode of a crime show that I like. I am always glad to see him, but not often that glad. It had been a great time by myself, but I was ready to hear about how he didn't eat much because his arm was occupied around the girl and how he had walked her home (she lives hear our house) first and that he couldn't wait to do it again soon. I heard that it was fun with the other friends and that he enjoyed the movie.

Foolishly I had thought that parenting only involved watching the children grow and change on a daily basis. Before that night, I never thought about the changes in me in response to the growth of the children. But as with every move we've made or new job I've taken, I will now be aware of the need to be flexible and at times, maybe even reinvent myself. It's all part of the journey that my son—and daughter—and I are taking together.

Dr. Aimee Weinstein (TokyoWriter.com) is a writer and writing professor who has lived eight out of the last ten years in Tokyo, Japan. She received her doctorate from the Department of Higher Education at George Mason University and has held positions at Temple University Japan, The George Washington University, and George Mason University. She has taught a variety of writing courses, from freshman composition to advanced expository writing. Her work has been published in Kaleidescope, Tokyo Weekender, inTouch, and Asian Jewish Life. She also maintains a regular blog where she fondly observes Tokyo life through the eyes of an American expat and writes about writing. Aimee currently resides in Tokyo with her supportive husband and two beautiful children, where she continues to write and help others in their writing.

My Grandfather's Determination

By DEBORAH FIKE (Eugene, Oregon) 18 October 2011

"Determination" is a word we throw around to indicate grand success. Athletes channel determination into their championship victories. Entrepreneurs transform determination into cash. Artists harness determination to go against the grain and follow their passion. "Determination" wraps itself in the stuff of legend — altering politics, discovering new worlds, and affecting millions of lives.

Determination also makes a single tomato plant grow.

My grandfather harnesses the kind of determination that doesn't make catchy news headlines. "Man Grows Tomatoes" isn't a tagline that will be celebrated by the Associated Press. Yet I can vouch for his determination. Grandpa can grow plants in the desert; it was his job as a farmer for more than 60 years. Now that he's retired, he only commands a half acre in his backyard, compared to the hundreds of acres he used to tend.

Nevertheless, you can't help but marvel at his personal garden, standing literally next to sagebrush. To make it work, Grandpa gets out of bed every morning around dawn, checks the day's weather, and adjusts his growing strategy accordingly. He drags garden hoses across his lawn and sets them up for optimal coverage. He harvests when he can, and he gives most of his yield away — to family, friends, and neighbors he's known since Franklin D. Roosevelt was president.

Not that FDR did a whole lot to help Grandpa out. By authorizing Executive Order 9066, President Roosevelt sent more than 100,000 Japanese Americans like my grandfather into internment camps. This did not deter Grandpa from joining the army, where he honed his Japanese language skills to become a radio operator. It also did not lessen my grandfather's pride in his country. He went on to become very active in his local veteran's group and still helps put little American flags on veteran gravestones every Memorial Day. He takes great pride in these small labors, barely noticed by most of his countrymen.

But true determination comes in the form of a life-threatening medical diagnosis. After nine decades, my grandfather has said good-bye to most of his generation, many of his friends suc-

 In our lives, we look up to people who wield determination to meet lofty goals. Our heroes live in the stories we read and the posters we hang on our walls. But sometimes, a hero is closer to us than we think.

cumbing to cancer. He routinely attends 2 funerals a month. So when the doctors tell my family that he has prostate cancer, we set our expectations accordingly. Hope for the best, but fear for the worst.

Grandpa, however, doesn't get the memo that life might be over. He very matter-of-factly tells the doctor to "fix it," the way you tell a barber to cut your hair. Even after preliminary tests look grim, he pushes for surgery. Many physicians won't operate on an 89-year-old man, especially if it looks like he only has six months to live. But Grandpa is in otherwise excellent health and in fact, had successfully undergone surgery two years previous. My grandfather goes under the knife.

To all of our surprise, the cancer hasn't spread as far as feared. The surgeon removes all the tumors, saving one biopsy for the lab. It will take several days, but the surgeon is hopeful that Grandpa will come out of this cancer free.

You would think that alone would be enough for my grandfather, but instead Grandpa has just one worry—he wants to go home. An argument ensues. The doctor wants Grandpa to stay under observation for at least 5 days. Grandpa won't hear of it. A bargain is struck—when my grandfather can walk, he will be discharged from the hospital. The moment the nurses turn their backs, he is on his feet, dragging his IV up and down the hospital corridors. Some of the nurses can't even keep up with him. He's back at home within 72 hours of surgery.

It should come to no surprise that a few days later, the doctor gets the lab results and officially declares Grandpa in remission. My grandfather doesn't even seem surprised. He knew he'd be fine all along.

In our lives, we look up to people who wield determination to meet lofty goals. Our heroes live in the stories we read and the posters we hang on our walls. But sometimes, a hero is closer to us than we think. When I had an emergency C-section this year, I didn't think of athletes, entrepreneurs or artists. I thought about Grandpa. And as I struggled to my feet, I searched for his quiet determination that helped him get home.

Deborah Fike is a founder of Avalon Labs, which provides consultations and writing services for start-ups and online businesses. She has a background in project management and teaches at the University of Oregon.

At Age 102, Margaret Dunning Drives to College

By DEBRA EVE (Los Angeles, California) 05 February 2013

Margaret Dunning drives her 1930 Packard 740 Roadster to classic car shows. It's causing a hoopla across the Interwebs.

She's twenty years older than her car and just got a scholarship to college!

Margaret was born in 1910 on a dairy farm west of Detroit to Charles and Elizabeth "Bessie" Dunning.

It was a bygone era. Margaret reveled in motoring from a young age. When she was 8, Charles taught her to steer his Model T while he operated the controls. She soon conquered the farm's truck and tractor.

Having Henry Ford as a neighbor didn't hurt.

She remembers Ford fondly:

"Dad would come in and say: Well, Henry's outside and I've asked him to stay for dinner. Mom had made huckleberry pie and offered Henry some. He said that was his favorite pie—I think he was being polite, but he was marvelous just like that."

But at age 12, she got her driver's license out of necessity. Charles died and Bessie had arthritic feet. The Model T passed to Margaret.

Mother and daughter eventually gave up the farm. They moved to Plymouth, Michigan, where Bessie built the house where Margaret still lives.

Margaret graduated from Plymouth High School in 1929 and studied two years at the University of Michigan. She dropped out at the Depression's height because Bessie needed her in the family business.

70 Years of Service

During World War II, Margaret volunteered in Plymouth's Red Cross motor pool, driving a truck. After, she spent several decades in banking, starting on the bottom rung as a teller.

In 1947, Margaret purchased Goldstein's Apparel on Plymouth's Main Street. She renamed it Dunning's Department Store and sold it in 1968 for a tidy sum. Her next act, as her community's greatest philanthropist, began with endowments to the Plymouth District Library and its Historical Museum.

From 1962 to 1984, Margaret served on the board of Community Federal Credit Union, including 19 years as president. During her tenure, the Credit Union increased its assets from $1 million to $40 million. In 1989, the Board established the Margaret Dunning Scholarship Fund to honor her contributions to Plymouth.

Last month, Today.com featured her and her gorgeous Packard. "I love the old cars," she said. "I love the smell of gasoline. It runs in my veins." She waxed poetic about changing her own oil and spark plugs all these years.

The FRAM Group, an auto products manufacturer, noticed the article. In a special ceremony at the Plymouth Historical Museum, they presented her with a full scholarship to the University of Michigan, eighty years after she dropped out. She'll also get free auto parts for life.

"I'm very, very pleased about it. I feel that I've been granted a few years that other people do not have, and I am really very happy that I have this beautiful old world to live in."

What most versions of the story leave out—Margaret didn't need that scholarship. She's one of those "millionaires next door" and could have financed her own education. Clearly, the gesture itself touched her.

"I'll have to figure out just what I'll study, but it will be in business…I'm still running a business right now. It's a trust fund."

Back to that Gorgeous Roadster

Margaret bought it in 1949. She's given it four upholstery jobs and 22 coats of hand-rubbed lacquer. The Classic Car Club of America awarded it 100 points—it's only perfect score. In addition to the Roadster, she owns a 1966 Cadillac DeVille, a 1975 Cadillac Eldorado convertible, and a 1931 Model A. Her "everyday car" is a 2003 Cadillac DeVille.

Ninety-four years after learning to drive, Margaret still makes special road trips. Just last summer, she motored from Michigan to California at the invitation of Pebble Beach Concours d'Élégance. There, she chatted with Henry Ford III and Edsel Ford II, and shared her personal photos of Henry.

Bertha Benz, the woman who pioneered the world's first road trip in 1888, would be proud.

Debra Eve (laterbloomer.com) *is a proud late bloomer and possessor of many passions. At 36, she became an archaeologist. At 42, a martial arts instructor. At 46, she married the love of her life! Now she writes about fellow late bloomers while plotting her next grand adventure.*

Eulogy for My Grandfather

By JODI LOBOZZO AMAN (Rochester, New York) 01 June, 2012

A certain whistle announced my grandfather's arrival since I was a little girl. He whistled the exact same tune every night coming home from work when my uncle, my mother, and my aunt where growing up. He'd come down the pathway to the side door of the house, and just as he passed the kitchen window, he'd whistle.

The three of them felt elated by this sweet melody because it meant their father's loving attention had arrived. It literally meant love has arrived.

As far as I understand, there is an abundance of love in heaven. But when my grandfather arrived Home three days ago, I am quite certain even the love in heaven multiplied exponentially.

Love has arrived.

I think my grandfather had a very important mission for his 86 years on earth. His mission was to clean. But I am not just talking about cleaning spots out of clothes at United Dry Cleaners, where he worked. I am talking about cleansing his soul and cleansing all our souls. And he did this by embodying love. Today, I want to share with you a glimpse into how my grandfather embodied love in his life. And tell you a bit of how this legacy, touched the lives of so many people.

The great thing about love like this is that it is not limited

Quite the contrary, the more you share love the more it grows. It's like a cake full of candles, with one lighter, you can light as many candles as you want: the flame multiplies. This is how I think of Grandpa's love.

Grandpa brought his love to heaven, and he can still love us from where he is, and he left an abundance of love here in each one of us. The love that he shared will continue to grow for decades to come as we parent and grandparent our own children.

There is already evidence that it is working because all of his great grandchildren are kind hearted. My little cousin, Aiden, who is a spitting image of my grandfather, knows this joy of giving. When he visited he always brought a drawing to give to his Papa Tony. A few weeks ago, Aiden was visiting excited to give Grandpa his drawing du jour, but Grandpa was sleeping. Grandpa made a little noise and Aiden ran for his paper, only to find that Grandpa didn't fully wake up. His persistence is exemplary, because this happened over and over and Aiden would get just as excited each time, finally rewarded when Papa Tony did wake up and fussed over his picture.

Grandpa wanted us to remember to do the right thing, because over and over he repeated his own father's words: "Always try to do the right thing." Even two weeks ago when Aunt Mary said to him, "Dad, I am so sorry you don't feel well, is there anything I can do?" My grandfather was still imparting this wisdom. He answered, "Just do the right thing."

Thank you God for another day so that I may help someone

Another way Grandpa expressed his love was by helping people. He loved to help people. His daily mantra was "Thank you God for another day so that I might help someone." Isn't this beautiful?

Even if he didn't feel good, he said this everyday, out loud, as he got out of bed or pulled on his pants. And he did not wait passively for someone to arrive needing help. He asked and he offered. He went out of his way to make sure people felt like they could count on him. He would tell his sister Florence, "Call me if you need anything, call me if the kids need anything."

He went often to the senior center and one day, barely being able to walk securely himself, he held the door for a man with a walker as he and Aunt Mary were leaving. Do you know, he walked the man all the way to his car and helped him in?

He loved beauty and expressed this. Recently, Mom was sleeping over and Grandpa came into her room in the middle of the night and was telling her how beautiful she looked tonight as he tucked the covers around her. One day when we were playing rummy, he said: "Jodi, Ted's sister Cathy is so beautiful." I think he saw holiness in us that sometimes we couldn't see in ourselves.

Grandpa knew how to express his love physically. He'd bend down to greet us with a big bear hug and plant loud kisses on our cheeks. His arms were always around his family.

In the last ten years, the Alzheimer's had him repeatedly playing the same few songs on the harmonica and the piano. Like Silent Night. The song must have had special significance to him, since it stayed in his head despite his clouded memory. Sometimes he would even murmur, "sleep in heavenly peace" or just "heavenly peace" as he walked around the house to bring himself comfort.

Laughter is the best medicine

One of Grandpa's greatest loving legacies was his sense of humor. He put people at ease immediately with his one liners, and kept them laughing. Like, "That food looks good enough to eat!" "I'd better sleep with my glasses on so I can see my dreams." "I'm pretty good shape for the shape I'm in", "Is that a left handed spoon?", "Did you get a haircut or did you get them all cut?", "At least I'm not old and crabby. I'm old but not crabby!" and "You'd better answer that it might be the telephone?" If you didn't respond with an appreciative giggle, he nudge you and repeat the joke to make sure you got it.

Grandpa loved to laugh. Whenever he made a mistake, instead of getting frustrated, he'd just laugh at himself. He did a belly giggle with his tongue between his teeth like the big kid that he was. He made so many funny mistakes that this kept him chuckling. His kids definitely acquired this sense of humor. When they were caring for him at the end, they would joke about who was doing what. If Aunt Mary was giving him a shot, she'd say "Dad, Joanne's giving you a shot now." Or vise versa, someone would be feeding him ice cream and across the room, Uncle Mike would yell, "Dad it's Mike, I'm giving you ice cream."

Hun

Grandma and Grandpa shared a beautiful relationship. He was deeply appreciative of her. He'd call her "My bride", saying "Isn't she beautiful, she's so beautiful, I love her so much, she does everything for me." And she did do everything for him. My grandmother gave him ten extra years through her care in checking his blood sugar, giving him healthy food, keeping him company. She gave him joy.

Grandma and Grandpa never called each other Tony and Nan. They called each other "Hun". Always! My cousins and I used to joke about it when we were little. We thought they both had the same first name. Even when they argued they called each other "Hun". They were so devoted to loving one another. They were always together and Grandpa did not want to go anywhere without her. He'd miss her dearly when she went out shopping or to the hairdresser, asking after her. He felt so safe in her care. She worked so hard and she too, knew how to do it right.

You're probably thinking, Jodi is just saying "love, love, love, love, love, love, love."

Yep, I am. This is the only way I can sum up my grandfather's life.

Love. Love. Love. Love. Love. Love. Love.

Wouldn't it be great if we could all sum up our life that way?

The last moments of Anthony Michael Julian's life were beautifully peaceful with his family's arms around him. Now, I imagine Grandpa putting his arms around all of us, always staying near.

Whenever we left a party, we would kiss Grandpa to say goodbye. He would always correct us. "Never say goodbye it's too final. Just say 'So long' or 'See you later'". "Goodbye" to my grandfather meant disconnection to those he loved. And he knew that even when we left each other physically, we can still stay connected to him. Curious, I researched the phrase "So long" and found out it was adapted into English from the Arabic word, "Salaam" meaning peace. How perfect is that?

Peace.

So long, Grandpa. See you later in heavenly peace.

Jodi Aman (jodiaman.com) *is a counselor, author, teacher, healer, mother, lover, friend, with over two decades of experience helping children, families, and individuals eliminate suffering. She has dedicated her life to helping others heal physically, emotionally, mentally, and spiritually, by loving them, inspiring them, and helping them create a new reality.*

Is Your Door Open?

By CATHRYN WELLNER (Kelowna, British Columbia) 16 September 2011

When Aunt Grace moved into a seniors care home, we all held our breaths. We expected her to hate it.

She had run her own life with no-nonsense efficiency and was quite happy to step in if someone else had trouble running theirs. She was also the soul of generosity. Where would she find outlets for her take-charge personality, her confident independence, and her endless generosity in a facility where someone else wrote the rules?

Uncle Dewey was dead. So was her son, Dewey, Jr. Her only surviving sister and her granddaughter lived far away. So did my brother and I. She had no interest in uprooting from the town where she had lived for decades.

Years of excess weight had taken their toll. Aunt Grace needed a walker for mobility. A residential facility was her only option. She seemed surprisingly sanguine about the prospect of moving into one room. At least the home was familiar. She had visited friends in it for years.

By this time she had already sold her home and given away much of her small accumulation of material goods. In her seventies she had started working as a live-in caregiver for elderly people. She was eighty when looking after people in their late eighties and nineties became too much for her.

With little fanfare or regret, Aunt Grace pared the rest of her belongings down to what would fit in one room. She moved into the care home, and we all held our breaths.

During the settling-in period, Aunt Grace was striding down the hallway with her walker when she saw a man shuffling along ahead of her. The home's activity director described what happened next.

"You!" Aunt Grace called out, not knowing the gentleman's name.

The old man stopped and peered over his shoulder. Aunt Grace gave one of her she-who-will-be-obeyed looks and said, "You get in your room and take off those trousers!"

In years of gradual decline, the old man had never once had a woman tell him to take off his trousers. He looked startled but went into his room and closed the door.

Aunt Grace waited outside the door. When it remained closed,

 "Leave it ajar," she called. "There are a lot of old people in here, and sometimes they need someone to talk to in the middle of the night."

she banged on it.

The old man opened it a few inches. "I told you to take off those trousers," Aunt Grace insisted.

Aunt Grace waited again, certain this time her order would be heeded.

When it wasn't, she banged again. The door opened slightly, and my aunt shook her finger at the frightened old man.

"Now you listen to me," she said. "We may be old in here, but we've got our pride. Your trousers are dragging on the ground. Take them off, and I'll fix them for you."

Next time the door opened, a thin arm handed out a pair of trousers. My aunt, who had brought along her sewing machine, hemmed them to a respectable length.

That was the start of her new enterprise in the care home. She hemmed trousers, let out seams, mended tears, and patched holes. She figured out how to hook a bag to her walker and offered laundry service for those who were no longer mobile enough to use the facility's washer and dryer.

Aunt Grace became such a beloved fixture in the home that

when I joined her for lunch during one of my rare visits to my childhood hometown, her table regulars were disappointed by her abandoning them for the visitor's table.

That visit was my last. She had become less mobile so had moved from the side of the facility where people could come and go freely to the side where people were too disabled to travel farther than the nearest hospital…or graveyard.

We talked and laughed for hours. I slipped her a hamburger and milkshake. "I'm 84, for heaven's sake. Does my doctor think I'll live forever if he starves me?"

Visiting hours ended at eight. "Close the door," she said.

We talked another two hours. By then she was looking tired. As I left her room, I turned out the light and started to pull the door shut behind me.

"Leave it ajar," she called. "There are a lot of old people in here, and sometimes they need someone to talk to in the middle of the night."

I never saw Aunt Grace again. She died shortly after my last visit. But sometimes, when disappointment, hurt or anger overtake me, I think of Aunt Grace. I remember her acceptance of whatever life brought her, her deep love for the people around her, and her unfailing generosity. I miss her unconditional love.

Is your door open, Aunt Grace? I need to talk.

Cathryn Wellner's meandering career path (thisgivesmehope.com; catchingcourage.com) has included stints as a French teacher, a school librarian, an itinerant storyteller, a university instructor, an arts organizer, a community developer, a communications consultant, a farmer and rancher, and a project manager. She is a citizen of two countries and has lived in five. The upside of all that change is stories. Now she has settled down to write them.

PART 4: OBSTACLES TO OVERCOME

"Success is to be measured not so much by the position that one has reached in life as by the obstacles which he has overcome."
                                                    - Booker T. Washington

Clearing Out the Weeds (In the Garden of Our Life)

By SHARON REED (Davidson, North Carolina) 15 February 2012

Some people are fair-weathered gardeners. They plant in spring and enjoy the view in the summer, only to ignore the garden the rest of the year. For them, gardening amounts to a weekend trip to the local garden center, five flats of flowers, and a bag of mulch. One afternoon's worth of planting and voila! An instant garden and the immediate gratification of flowers already in bloom.

I used to be that kind of gardener. Oh sure — I descend from a long lineage of good gardening stock and often thought of myself as having proudly inherited a green thumb. How wrong was I! What I acquired was an appreciation of others' efforts...of the end result...of the idea of gardening. I could weed and till and plant with the best of them — for one day, for one month, for one season. Just don't ask me to maintain. But good gardening, like a good life, requires on-going attention and maintenance, like it or not.

I took one look at the first signs of spring in my new garden, and could plainly see what had been hidden in the full bloom of summer when I first stumbled upon my cottage. Weeds. Lots of them. Some of them small, resting shallowly upon the surface; others of them big and deeply rooted. Some even have flowers of their own, often confusing to the inexperienced gardener, but weeds none the less, threatening to crowd out and suffocate the new life emerging from the good stock of the garden. More than I could tackle in a day, more than I could pull out in a week. Signs of spring still beginning to emerge amidst the weeds, I thought to myself, "this is going to take a while."

Isn't that how it is with our own baggage sometimes?

We try and plant new seeds and establish new gardens, without first clearing out the weeds and preparing the soil. Sometimes we're successful, but only for a season or two. When we fail to cut back, clear out, and prepare for the new, the baggage of our hearts often crowd out new blooms, overshadowing or diluting the long term health and vitality of our lives. Eventually, if left untended, the weeds will overtake the beauty of the present, the untilled soil too hard to accommodate new life.

So today I started a new project. Weeding. Deliberate, sometimes difficult, always time-consuming. Digging and pulling, pulling and tilling. The thing is — not only is the act of weeding often cathartic in and of itself, but the time, effort, and pain involved always paves the way to new, healthier growth…to

 But good gardening, like a good life, requires on-going attention and maintenance, like it or not.

a bountiful and beautiful garden…to a stronger and wiser gardener.

Yes, it is a season of the hard work of gardening. Of excavating the old and preparing for the new. And in this season, I will learn to find joy in the hard work itself. I will resist the temptation to cut corners and create an 'instant' garden. I will work joyfully in remembrance that life's seasons are always changing and we must change and grow with them; in the certain knowledge that an untended garden will first grow unruly and then wither and die from neglect; and with the wisdom that if we live only for the beauty of spring and summer, we miss the important lessons of the fall and winter of our lives.

Just as the mountain calls us to stretch our reach and to persevere through the struggle, so, too, does the garden teach us the value and importance of routine maintenance and the secrets of the seasons. Don't you just love how Mother Nature provides us with all of the lessons we will ever need, right here in our own back yard?

Sharon Reed (heartpath.wordpress.com) is a global and civic-minded strategist who writes and speaks on living and leading a heart-aligned life. She is passionate about building bridges of understanding and empowering others to make a positive difference in the world – through communication, connection, education and engagement. Sharon is also the founder and chief editor of the Global Girls Project, a collaborative writing project dedicated to empowering women and girls around the world through stories of heart-aligned leadership (www.globalgirlsproject.org). Sharon lives in Davidson, NC with her two children, Michael and Allison.

Lessons Learned From Being Bullied

By COLLEEN CANNEY (Seattle, Washington) 09 May 2013

During my middle school years, I had the experience of being bullied. At the time, the term "bullying" wasn't as readily used as it is today. To me, the situation was just viewed as one that entailed being the target for a group of popular girls. Walking down the hall brought about extreme anxiety as I wondered, "What verbal onslaughts will be thrown my way today?" I was also harassed because of my grades. One day for example, my History teacher posted our grades outside the classroom door and someone wrote, "Brown Noser," beside my name because I received an A. After that experience, I remember hiding exam grades for fear of being taunted.

The bullying situation hit a climax right before my 8th grade graduation. The leader of the popular girl pack, a tall blonde who caused me the most grief, threatened to beat me up. As a result of this scare tactic, I hid in my closet and never attended my 8th grade graduation. This was the first time I "skipped" school but at the time, I didn't see any other alternative. As a rather shy and petite individual, I couldn't fathom going head-to-head with an extremely intimidating girl twice my size. I had no idea what it meant to fight and I sure didn't want to find out.

8th grade graduation caused me to see my situation in desperate terms. The thought of going through high school with these mean girls constantly harassing me was not something I wanted to sign-up for. The day after I hid in my closet, I talked, or rather begged, my parents to send me to another school outside of our district. Luckily my parents had the financial means to pay for a private school so during the summer before freshman year of high school, I enrolled in a Catholic high school about 30 miles from my house.

During my freshman year at the private high school I attended, I remember standing in the cafeteria when a wave of anxiety came over me. I was having flashbacks of being bullied and found myself nervously peering around me, wondering if someone was going to start yelling choice words at me or give me "if looks could kill" glares. Then a wave of relief came over me and I realized that no one was paying any attention to me (in a good way!). At this point

When we do find this strength, the universe will help us see the path we are meant to follow.

I realized there was no need to live in fear at school anymore. I was safe in my new school and I could let my guard down.

High school turned out to be a completely different experience for me than middle school. I thrived in the strong academic environment the private school fostered and found that I "fit" with my fellow studious classmates who also loved school and were driven to excel. In high school I no longer had to hide from who I truly was but instead I could simply just be.

The question of why I became the target for bullying perplexed me for some time. After a number of years of contemplation however, my conclusion is that I didn't fit the mold for the homogenous community that I grew up in. It seemed as though these girls picked-up on the fact that I wasn't going to conform to the standard norm and my quiet defiance threatened their collective power. I didn't dress like them, think like them, and didn't strive to be like them, even though they were the so-called "popular girls." While I was fairly insecure as a result of being bullied, I still clung to my strong sense of self that wanted to fully emerge.

From my experience of being bullied, I learned a few different lessons that may help others who have experienced bullying:

1. Deep within every person there is a well of courage – Being bullied has given me confidence to stand firm in who I am and what I believe in. Being a follower in life will only get you so far and will really limit your way of thinking. It's important to forge your own identity in life, even if it means going against the norm. When we develop an authentic sense of self-confidence, we no longer question who we are.

2. Don't waste time on individuals who don't accept you – In life we may meet a few or many individuals who simply don't like us for whatever reason and while this fact may be hard to accept, once we do accept it, we will be more at peace in life. Instead of going through trying to gain approval from others, we simply just need to remain true to ourselves and have compassion and empathy for others, even those who reject us.

3. During our darkest hours light will eventually emerge – When we are in the midst of seemingly unbearable pain, we may feel as though our situation is hopeless and we may struggle to see a way out. What we must remember however is that each of us has a tremendous amount of tenacity within us and miraculously we can find the strength to overcome adversity. When we do find this strength, the universe will help us see the path we are meant to follow. Lightness will then overtake the darkness that has been suffocating us.

Colleen Canney (colleencanney.com) is a Career and Spiritual Leadership Coach with clients around the world. Colleen brings a well-rounded background that includes an MBA and over ten years' experience working as a Human Resources professional in both the private and non-private sectors.

Watch Out for that Rough Section Ahead

By LAURA BEST (East Dalhousie, Nova Scotia) 24 October 2011

If you have traveled the back roads in Nova Scotia, you're bound to have seen a few road signs that warn of a rough section ahead unless you're watching the scenery and not paying close attention to road signs. (Can't say as I'd blame you if you were.)

For anyone not familiar with the road ahead such warning signs are probably a welcome thing, although I've noticed that not all sections that are rough and full of potholes come with this warning. Sometimes bumps and potholes spring from out of nowhere, and you're left travelling the back roads at your own risk. Still, the sign is a good idea. It warns us to adjust our speed and take it easy.

All summer I've mused over a particular sign on my way to and from work. Some "rough section" signs let the driver know just how lengthy the rough section is. The one I pass by, however, does not. Luckily, it doesn't mean that the potholes and bumps go on forever. Being familiar with the road, I know that the rough section is only a few kilometers long and I'll be rewarded at the end by a section of new pavement.

Earlier this summer I hit a rough section in my writing. I was working on a particular chapter that wasn't going the way I'd hope, but each day, as I passed that sign, I reminded myself that this was something that all writers experience from time to time. I often tell people that Bitter, Sweet seemed to write itself. Each day that I sat down to write, the words were right there. There were times when I felt as though I was simply recording a story that already existed because the characters felt so real. Little wonder I was surprised to find that rough section waiting for me this summer.

As writers, we all travel a different road. Sometimes that road is level and we go along at a decent speed. But other times the road is uneven. Finding our way through to the end is not always an easy thing. Some writers plough through their first draft. Once they make it through to the end they go back and take out all the bumps and holes they left behind in their wake. I've never been that kind of writer. I have to fix the potholes along the way. I have to smooth out the rough sections as I go along often times revising a particular section again and again until I can read it aloud without hearing any awkward or misplaced words. For me, the words in each sentence needs a particular rhythm that comes from having just the right amount of words and syllables.

Looking back now, as difficult as what that rough section was to get through, it felt mighty good to eventually emerge on the other side. We really don't need to concern ourselves over every rough section we come up against. Whether or not we have any warning will make little difference to our writing. The important thing to remember is that all rough sections eventually come to an end and when they do we can travel along and enjoy the beautiful scenery for awhile.

Laura Best (laurabest.wordpress.com) *has had over forty short stories published in literary magazines and anthologies. Her first young adult novel, "Bitter, Sweet," was short listed for the Geoffrey Bilson Award for Historical Fiction for Young People and made the Best Books for Kids and Teens 2011 list. Her second novel, "Flying With A Broken Wing" is soon to be released.*

The Beat of a Different Drum

By CAROLYN SOLARES *(Minneapolis, Minnesota) 30 May 2011*

After eating Chinese one day last summer, I opened a fortune cookie that contained a fortune strange enough that it has stuck with me for months: **Next summer you will march to the beat of a new drum.** I have eaten at many Chinese restaurants and opened countless fortune cookies in my life, but never have I received a fortune that contained a specific timeframe. And while I have been known to pin especially fun ones on my fridge or bulletin board, I don't normally ascribe much significance to them.

This particular fortune, however, grabbed my attention and my imagination. For days following my Chinese lunch, I speculated on what this portent might mean. I had spent the better part of the previous five years discovering who I was and learning to really live. What would change in my life by next (now this) summer? What was the new beat I'd be marching to? I imagined all sorts of possibilities about what my future and fortune might hold.

For many years, I had lived a busy, but gloomy life, believing that my heartache and misery were unique. (They weren't.) Somewhere along the way, I began to hear a drum beating, albeit faintly at first, telling me that everyone's story contains some heartbreak and grief. Then, more loudly, this rhythm chided me gently, but firmly, "Get over yourself. Be happy!"

Be happy? Honestly, it had never occurred to me. But nothing else had worked, I reasoned. So, why not try? Let me be clear that this was not an overnight transformation. Over the past few years, there have been high-highs and low-lows as I learned what happy looked like, and more importantly, felt like. I had to overcome entrenched habits. I had to create room to breathe and tune in to the wise beat that called to me.

As May rolls into June, with signs of summer around the corner, I have been thinking about the curious message I received nearly a year ago. With so many positive changes in my life over the previous five years, I foolishly believed last summer that I had made it to an end game. But in hindsight, I was marching to many drums. Too many. At best, the cacophony of varying opinions, beliefs, and advice was confusing. It was also very loud.

I couldn't think and I couldn't breathe. Finally, in a defiant act that turned out to be self-preservation, I abruptly tuned out all of the competing opinions and conflicting advice that just didn't feel right. The silence was startling and stark.

Then I heard a familiar beat, one I had been drowning out. The more attentively I listened, the clearer it became, beating a steady rhythm that resonated through me with clarity and truth: I had outgrown my life. It was changing again, but I was reluctant to change and grow with it.

With new understanding, I started to pay attention to the nudges, the hunches, not to mention the pit in my stomach, that were all trying to help me hear the only beat that mattered. With a sad and heavy heart, I ended a friendship. To my great surprise, I felt both relief and freedom. I had spent months trying to dissect this relationship, only to realize that its chaotic tempo was making me crazy.

Feeling five-hundred pounds lighter, I knew with certainty that I could trust this drum with its guiding, steady, and powerful beat. I dusted off my own creativity, ideas, and beliefs, which sent new rhythm reverberating through me with purpose and strength.

So much has changed in my life since last summer. While it wasn't all easy, it has all been good. Really, really good. I now know that there is no "end-game" in living a happy life. Change is constant — and being happy entails embracing change and infinite opportunities to grow.

I am indeed now marching to the beat of a different drum: my own. But it's not new; it's the drum that has been beating steadily and melodically my entire life. And this summer, I am thankfully smart enough to recognize everything else as just noise.

Living with Depression: A Personal and Professional View

By DEBORAH SERANI, (New York, New York), 31 October 2011

As a young girl, I always felt this looming sense of sadness. I remember feeling tired and sullen a good deal of the time when I was in school. These feelings didn't get much better when I was at home either. Like Eeyore, the glum little donkey from the Hundred Acre Wood, sometimes family and friends saw me as a sad-sack. Unaware of what depression was or how to detect it, I descended into a Major Depressive Episode when I was a 19 year old college student, back in 1980. Hopeless and suicidal, I nearly took my life with a handgun. Luckily, my attempt was interrupted, and swift medical help was sought. I found a psychologist who helped release me from the grip of my unshakable sadness and taught me about the mood disorder called Unipolar Depression. Not only did psychotherapy save my life, it inspired me to become a student of its practice.

In the following years of my depressive episode, I finished college, went to graduate school, obtained a doctoral degree in psychology, fell in love, and married—all while continuing psychotherapy. Through talk therapy, I learned how my unique life history, experiences, and specific traumas influenced the way I thought, felt, behaved, and ultimately shaped who I was as a young woman. The insight I gained was life changing and life saving. I applied the learned skills and techniques whenever difficulties presented. And they did—many times over. I never fell into a deep depression.

That is, until 1993, just shortly after the birth of my daughter.

And it was good that I studied many years as a psychologist, learning about mental illness in all its forms. I was better prepared to deal with my second major depressive episode, swiftly recognizing its Postpartum onset. I knew about neurobiology and research on antidepressants, and willingly accepted the idea of taking medication to treat my depression. With adding medication to my treatment plan, I began to feel better in a matter of weeks.

But not only did I feel better. . . I felt better than ever.

For the first time in my life, there was an effortless way of just being. I no longer felt the heaviness of gravity. There was an ease to the tempo of my day that never existed before. It was a dramatic experience for me because I came to realize that I wasn't just recovering from my second depressive episode. I became painfully aware that I was, indeed, depressed my entire life.

 I understood the shame patients experienced needing medication or how they felt betrayed by their body's neurobiological weaknesses.

Now, a therapist doesn't need to live through an event or have firsthand knowledge to help someone heal. However, the subjective experience of my mental illness, its long-standing trajectory, and my familiarity with medication informed me in ways that clinical training and education never could. I lived within the layers of depression and knew the identifiable, the indescribable, and the insidious textures of it. When working with children and adults, I was better able to recognize the roadblocks that came from neurobiological aspects of depression versus emotional resistance in the psychological sense. I understood the shame patients experienced needing medication or how they felt betrayed by their body's neurobiological weaknesses. I could relate to the stories of frustration from side effects and to the decisions to stop medication because side effects were intolerable.

My emotional journey has taken me from sadness to despair, through adversity to resolve. Through it all, I discovered within myself hidden reserves of strength and spirit—what many in the field call resilience. Writing about depression and advocating for those who experience mental illness have become the silver lining of my depressive cloud. I've been a go-to expert for the psychological issues of depression for many media outlets including Newsday, Psychology Today, The Chicago Sun Times, Glamour Magazine, The Associated Press, and affiliate radio station programs at CBS and NPR, just to name a few. Now in full remission for almost 15 years, I use my personal experiences with depression to inform my clinical work as a therapist. This dual approach gives me a unique perspective because not only do I know what it's like to diagnose and treat depression... I know what it's like to live with it too.

It is my hope that my story of living with depression will serve as an encouraging reminder that depression can be treated—and that there's no shame living with mental illness.

Dr. Deborah Serani (drdeborahserani.com) is the author of "Living with Depression: Why Biology and Biography Matter along the Path to Hope and Healing" by Rowman & Littlefield Publishers. She is a practicing psychologist and adjunct professor in New York City, and has worked as a technical advisor for the television show Law & Order: Special Victims Unit.

Sometimes, You Just Have to Say No

By CATHRYN WELLNER (Kelowna, British Columbia) 12 June 2011

For over twenty years my mother did the bookkeeping for a seed company in Twin Falls, Idaho. The salary was low. Hours were long. She worked five and a half days a week and never got more than a couple weeks of vacation.

I don't know if she loved the job. I do know she was loyal and hard working. She was a bright woman who earned every bit of praise that came her way. She never complained about working conditions. She was proud of her position in the company.

There were few perks, but there was one we loved. The company had a trial ground where they grew the vegetables they were experimenting with. New varieties of corn, beans, and peas were their specialty. When they finished their tests and assessments, they invited employees to glean any corn left on the stalks. Most didn't bother, but we stocked up for winter.

That was before the days of corn that stays sweet no matter how many days have passed since it was picked. We would fill the pot before heading to the trial ground with our gunny sacks. August was always hot and sunny, but visions of sweet kernels bursting on our tongues kept us picking every possible ear.

We would load the bulging sacks into the car, drive home, and turn on the stove. While the water heated, we would husk enough corn for dinner and slice a few tomatoes from our garden.

That was dinner. What more do you need when corn is ripe and tomatoes are at their peak? Some salt, a bit of butter. Heaven is in the eating.

The seed company's small salary kept Mother, my brother, and me afloat through elementary school, junior high, and right through our graduation. Mother would have stayed until she retired, but my brother moved away, married, and started a family. The lure of grandchildren trumped job loyalty.

So Mother turned in her resignation. I'm sure she felt a twinge, after so many years with the company.

They advertised for her replacement. I don't know how many people the company interviewed. I do know they found someone and asked Mother to train him.

Her bookkeeping job was reclassified to a managerial level, with the same tasks but a dramatically increased salary. Until then, I doubt Mother had ever questioned the position she held in the company. She was happy to have a good job and occasional raises. Money was always tight, but she never complained. She worked five and a half days a week, seldom took a sick day and managed to keep us in food and rented housing.

Still, my mother was a strong believer in social justice. Being asked to train a well-paid manager to do the job she had done as an underpaid clerk violated her sense of what was right.

And so she said no. I admire her for that. It took a lot of courage for someone as loyal and hard working, with years of stellar service, to look the boss she liked in the eye and tell him she would not train her replacement because the whole thing was unfair.

I'm sure he was taken aback. This friendly, competent woman, who always did what she was asked, and did it well, drew a line in the sand.

The episode cast a shadow over her years with the seed company, but she didn't spend the rest of her life in bitter memories. She moved on. She found other work, which also paid poorly, and once again did it well.

Mother was one of the most sociable and contented people I have ever known. She had more important things to do than nurse regrets. There were, after all, grandchildren to love.

Cathryn Wellner's *meandering career path (thisgivesmehope.com; catch-ingcourage.com) has included stints as a French teacher, a school librarian, an itinerant storyteller, a university instructor, an arts organizer, a community developer, a communications consultant, a farmer and rancher, and a project manager. She is a citizen of two countries and has lived in five. The upside of all that change is stories. Now she has settled down to write them.*

It's Hard to Lose Something You Love

By *CARRIE ELLEN BRUMMER (Dubai, United Arab Emirates) 26 May 2011*

Indeed, it is hard to lose something you love.

That "something" could be a family member, a friendship, a relationship, and many other scenarios. In all of these moments it is raw. It really hurts. You can feel like your whole world is falling to pieces and the hopes and dreams you had for that something are all gone.

When we are in the middle of emotional moments and times, here's my advice (as an artist and teacher)… CREATE! Some of the greatest artwork, poems, and songs have come from dark moments and sad places. What an opportunity to channel negativity into something concrete to face it, accept it, and eventually move forward.

Strategies for channeling creative energies in hard times

1. Take photos of your beloved deceased or ex-partner and incorporate them into a collage artwork or mixed media work. A few years ago I had a friend who shared with me that she incorporated her ex into all of her paintings when she was grieving. She placed him or symbols of him in funny places, as ugly evil clowns, etc. The same woman made a joke with me about my ex being Gollum (Lord of the Rings) so I drew him morphing into that creature. Boy did it feel good at the time!

2. Write letters to those you miss or to the dream you had that is now shattered. How many authors have used letters as creative fodder for their novels or stories!? You may not be able to use it now, but it could prove useful after the grieving is over. Besides, even if it doesn't it will help you release some negative energy while you are going through your hard time.

3. Journal, journal, journal. Drawing or writing, it doesn't

matter… when you are overwhelmed with your feelings it is good to get them out. It does help clear your head, I promise, I do it all the time!

4. Say yes to commissions and projects. Keeping busy will force you to be creative, and sometimes get your mind off of what is bothering you. It never hurts to take breaks from the pain you are experiencing!

The grieving process will end. Of course, while you are going through the grieving process you will still cry, hate, love, miss, dream, sigh, and repeat all of those emotions over and over again. But by allowing yourself to truly express those feelings, maybe you can move forward sooner and make some amazing artwork along the way!

It is easy in times of grief or sadness to be self-punishing. Do you want to move forward with your life? Then be certain to embrace your creativity more than ever when times are hard. You may have already lost something important to you, don't lose another integral part of your being. You deserve good things as do the people around you.

Special Note: If you find yourself wallowing in grief or cannot get out of your rut, or even have thoughts of self-harm, remember it is okay to seek help. PLEASE seek help. You have people who care about you and want to help, even if it doesn't feel like it. Family, friends, and counselors can all help you move forward with your life. Grief is a natural process that takes time but it will be easier if you let people help you move through it. I can tell you my family and friends have offered me that support more than once and each time I remember just how blessed and lucky I am!

Carrie Ellen Brummer (artistthink.com) is an artist, a teacher, and a dreamer. She has been teaching Visual Arts for 8 years to students who have enriched her life! Carrie is also a practicing artist who has had art exhibits in both the United States and Dubai.

How to Find Perspective in a Hard Moment

By BECKY ROBINSON (SE Michigan, Ohio) 24 August 2011

Early April and rain poured from the sky. I sat with my best friend's husband, Jason, in his car, waiting for the rain to let up a little. From where we sat, we could see huge puddles forming, a few brave souls walking toward the start line, dripping wet. Some wore garbage bags as raincoats.

For those few moments, we were still dry.

By the time the race started, the rain had mostly stopped, but we took off running with feet soaked to the skin.

I felt tired before I even started. I think (although I can't remember) that I had been up during the night with my two year old.

I knew (although I did not KNOW) that I was pregnant with my third child (a home pregnancy test would confirm it later that week.) In light of my pregnancy, I also knew this would be my last race for a while.

I knew that I had always wanted to run a race on Chicago's lakefront.

I knew the conditions were less than ideal.

I knew that I wanted to enjoy the race despite the rain, my wet feet, and the water dripping from my hair.

So, this is what I did: as I ran, I told myself that even though the race felt hard, it was nothing compared to two things, what I'd gone through before and what lay ahead.

This is nothing, I told myself, compared to the 8 months of pregnancy you have ahead of you. This is nothing, I told myself, compared to another C-section that awaits. This is nothing, compared to caring for a newborn. You think you feel tired now, I told myself — you will feel more tired than this, very soon.

I also raised my head so I could see the sun breaking through

INSPIRING HOPE — ONE STORY AT A TIME

the clouds, diamonds of light reflecting off Lake Michigan. In the present moment, I had what I needed.

I told myself: you can do this, and you will be strong for what comes next.

As I passed the nine mile mark, I saw the familiar faces of my husband and two daughters. I heard them cheering me. I kept running, picking up my pace in that 10th mile.

In every difficult moment, it is likely true that you have gone through something even more difficult before (and survived.) It is also likely true that you will go through something more difficult in the future.

In those two truths are strength for the present, difficult moment.

Perhaps this seems counter intuitive to you, this idea of reflecting on hard moments in your past as encouragement in whatever difficulty you now face. Perhaps it seems counter intuitive to project that you will face even bigger difficulties in your future.

I ask you to reflect on both the past and what is ahead because in between those two places is perspective.

You are strong enough to endure this.

You have endured before, you will endure again, and you can endure now.

In this present moment, you have all that you need.

Becky Robinson is a social media strategist, author and founder of weavinginfluence.com leading a team of more than 20 skilled professionals partnering with authors and thought leaders to grow their online influence and market their books. She formed Team Buzz Builder, a supportive community of bloggers that she mobilizes on behalf of authors. She also has an extensive network of online followers through the Twitter accounts @beckyrbnsn, @weaveinfluence, @teambuzzbuilder, and @teamfaithbuildr. Becky is the author of 12 Minutes to Change Your Day, Your Book Deserves a Celebration, and 31 Days of Twitter Tips: Grow Your Online Influence, 12 Minutes at a Time. She is a wife and mother of three daughters.

Living to Learn

"Live as if you were to die tomorrow.
Learn as if you were to live forever."
- Mahatma Gandhi

Follow Your Passion

By NINA MUNTEANU (Lunenburg, Nova Scotia) 05 May 2011

I'm a successfully published author with acclaimed novels, short stories and essays published all over the world. But I almost didn't get there. What if I told you that I never read as a kid, I was the worst speller in my school and I used bad grammar? I didn't excel in typing class and practically failed English 101.

Are you a storyteller? Because that's where it all starts. With a story. The rest is window dressing. Every author is on a journey, a hero's journey, really. Because that's what most writers are: heroes. We journey into the dark frightening abyss and return with the prize for the world: truth. The writer's life is not really romantic, like many believe. It is rife with doubt, rejection, betrayal and disappointment. But it is also graced with the richness of joy, satisfaction, energy and fulfillment. When a writer writes what he or she is passionate about, there is nothing better. Absolutely nothing. So, let me tell you a story now, about how I almost didn't become a writer but did because it was what I had to do. Like most stories, this one has a beginning, middle and an end...

The Beginning: The Sweet Promise

When I was ten years old, I knew what I wanted to be when I grew up: I was going to be a paperback writer. It was 1964 and I'd taken my favorite rock group's song to heart, the Beatles' "I Want to be a Paperback Writer". It was an incredible moment of clarity for me and despite being challenged by my stern and unimaginative primary school teacher, who kept trying to corral me into being "normal", I wasn't going to let anyone stem my creativity and eccentric — if not wayward — approach to literature, language and writing. I was a confident, but lovable, little brat and I knew it.

As a teenager, I wrote, directed and recorded "radio plays" with my sister. When we weren't bursting into riotous laughter, it was actually pretty good. She and I shared a bedroom in the back of the house and at bedtime we opened our doors of imagination to a cast of thousands. We fed each other wild stories of adventure and intrigue, murmuring and giggling well into the night long after our parents were snoring in their beds. Those days scintillated with liberating originality, excitement and joy. My hero was science fiction author and futurist, Ray Bradbury; I vowed to write profoundly stirring tales like he did. Stories that mattered. Stories that lingered with you long after you finished them. Stories that made you think and dream and changed you imperceptibly.

I had found what excites me — my passion for telling stories — and I'd inadvertently stumbled upon an important piece of the secret formula for success: 1) having discovered my passion, I decided on a goal; 2) I found and wished to emulate a "hero" who'd achieved that goal and therefore had a "case study"; 3) I applied myself to the pursuit of my goal. Oops… the third one, well…

…It went downhill from there. I grew up.

The Middle: The Struggles & Confusion of "Reality"

Recognizing my talent and interest in the visual arts and graphic design, my parents pushed me to get a fine arts degree in university and go into teaching or advertising. They made it obvious that fiction writing was not a viable career or a forté of mine. (I was lousy at spelling and, despite my ability to tell stories and my love for graphic novels, I didn't read books!) I can still remember my father's lecture about how perfect the teaching or nursing profession was for me. The second blow to my author-ego came in the form of a high school Career Aptitude Test, meant to prepare us for our career decisions. Secretly harboring my paperback novelist dream, I filled out my forms with great excitement. How deflating to find out that I was best suited to be a sergeant in the army! "Writing" as a career barely made it on the graph, and scored well below "computer programmer" and "mechanic".

I deferred to the "wisdom" of others and let myself be diverted and distracted by clever reasoning and an appeal to logic. I began to visualize a career in advertising. I did what I thought I should do, not what truly excited me.

I quietly held my dream of being a paperback novelist close to my heart. But self-expression had dwindled and in its empty wake I discovered a cause worth investing a fervent energy: the well-being of our planet. With the cause came my pursuit of a science degree. I left home and surprised and disappointed my parents by electing on registration day at the university to go into science rather than pursue a fine arts degree in advertising. Although I wasn't "expressing", I was nevertheless inspired. My Master's of Science degree, university teaching and technical writing proved worthwhile in eventually publishing hard-science fiction stories and novels of substance about the environment.

The End: Fulfillment

My non-fiction articles became my entrance into the world of fiction and I used this venue to polish my writing skills in fiction (don't let anyone tell you that non-fiction can't be exciting, bending to many of the same rules as in fiction writing). Once I began publishing fiction stories, I never looked back. And as far as I'm concerned, the sky's the limit now.

Not too long ago, I quit my day job and moved across the country to an artistic community on the east coast. I am currently travelling the world and pursuing my dream as a full-time author and writing coach. It's not an easy life. And it can be lonely at times. But it is so incredibly fulfilling and blessed with meaning. As a writing coach I get to help others realize their dreams too. Come, walk with me and pursue your dream. It's for the taking.

Nina Munteanu (ninamunteanu.com) has written several novels, short stories, and essays published worldwide and translated into several languages. Nina teaches and coaches writing through her website. Her acclaimed "The Fiction Writer: Get Published, Write Now!" is currently the textbook for creative writing classes at several universities and schools in North America.

5 Simple Steps to Achieve Your Goals

By KAARINA DILLABOUGH (Amaranth, Ontario) 28 August 2011

We complicate things... yes, we often make things far more complicated than they really are.

And what with the burgeoning amount of information, opportunity, challenge and choice that we have available to us, it's easy to feel like there aren't enough hours in the day, and only a super-hero could accomplish it all.

In actual fact, achieving one's goals rests on a foundation of thought, action, evaluation and recalibrating.

Step 1: decide2do

Before anything comes into being, it is preceded by a thought. When that thought is sufficiently important, you decide2do something about it. A decision is very different than a thought, however. It's been said that we average about 60,000 thoughts per day. We certainly don't decide2do 60,000 things per day! When a thought becomes a decision, that's the powerful motivator behind ACTION.

Step 2: Set priorities

Priorities are very different than a "to do" list. A "to do" list never gets "tuh dun"…it just keeps growing longer and longer. When you set priorities, you identify THE MOST IMPORTANT things, based on your decisions, to accomplish. And I suggest that setting a maximum of 3 to 5 priorities for each day (set the night before) is the maximum to strive for. Otherwise, you're just creating a "to do" list. These priorities are either objectives (stepping stones to your goals) or actual goals themselves.

Step 3: Follow-through and DO

Once you've decided and set priorities, the action step(s) should be clear. But this is where many fail. They've thought about something, decided it was important but not really prioritized it. When it isn't important enough, we just don't do it. So you might say it's important to get healthy, but you haven't really decided to get healthy. When the decision is made, the actions will align. Now that doesn't mean we won't get tempted, or stray from the path. But a true decision, identified as a priority will beg the actions to fulfill it. So: plan your priorities, don't prioritize your plan. And with Step 2, decide how you will evaluate success. We're really good at measuring outputs — the things we do. We're not so good at measuring outcomes — the results we achieve. Be sure to determine how you will measure results.

Step 4: Monitor and adjust as necessary

There's a saying that goes: "Write a plan. But the moment it's written, it's redundant." Yikes! So why write it in the first place? First, because writing makes it real. A plan in your head is no plan at all. And things will happen that you didn't anticipate. Things you thought would work might not. It's important to keep a finger on the pulse of your planned priorities, and adjust as circumstances require.

Step 5: Evaluate

What went well? What went awry? How will you measure results? There are as many qualitative and quantitative forms of measurement as there are stars in the sky. The metrics you'll use is something you'll decide upon when you set your priorities. Figure out at that stage "how" you'll measure results, and be sure to evaluate your results, or outcomes.

(Think - Decide - Set Priorities - Follow-through and DO - Monitor and adjust as necessary - Evaluate - Rinse and Repeat!)

Kaarina Dillabough (kaarinadillabough.com) is a business consultant, coach and strategist. Her high-voltage energy, passion, expertise and experience inspire those she works with to reach beyond their grasp, to attain great things in business and in life. As a former Olympic level coach, Kaarina applies the same approach to individuals as she did with athletes: lighting the fire within to help people see their true potential. A popular speaker, Kaarina has an engaging storytelling style that never fails to inform, educate and entertain. Her content is always fresh and full of value, as she combines a wealth of leading-edge information with her own unique point of view.

What Does Work-Life Balance Mean Anyway?

By COLLEEN CANNEY (Seattle, Washington) 13 March 2013

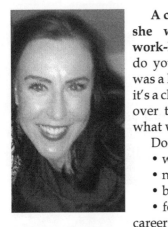

A coaching client contacted me because she wanted guidance on maintaining work-life balance. She asked me, "So, how do you achieve work-life balance?" There was a long pause and then I said, "Honestly, it's a challenge for me." With that being said, over the years I have had to think about what work-life balance means.

Does it mean:
- working only 40 hours per week
- never working outside of the office
- being able to set your own hours
- feeling fulfilled and energized in your career

My conclusion is that work-life balance should be defined by each individual person. The ideal work situation should be one in which you are excited to go to work and you don't feel completely drained by the end of the day. When you are truly passionate about what you do, work shouldn't seem like work. Call me an idealist but we spend far too much time at work to not love what we do.

With that being said, it's vital that people set boundaries with work. A woman once said to me, "You love to work because you don't allow work to control you."

So, how do we prevent work from overwhelming us? How can we stay energized at work instead of being consumed with fear and anxiety? Finally, how do we effectively recharge our batteries in order to ensure we approach work with optimal energy levels?

Here are some tips that may help with the above:

1. Get a handle on email both in terms of sending and receiving. Let's start with the emails you send. To quote Shakespeare, "Brevity is the soul of wit." What does this mean? Get to the point in as few words as possible and be empathetic to the reader of the email. At work, the majority of people aren't keen on having to read short stories that could be summed up in a few bullet points or a quick summary. Provide as much information that is needed and make sure your action items or questions are clearly stated. The most stressful type of email to receive is one that goes on and on and you are left wondering, what is the point of this email and did the sender decide to write a stream of consciousness email? In terms of managing the emails you receive, the best guidance I received at Microsoft is the one touch approach to email. This means you only look at an email once and do one of the following: 1) Delete – if the email didn't pertain to you or it was a read only email that did not require any action on your part 2) Take Action – if a response is needed, there is no time like the present to answer the email and then delete it. Now, taking action can be a bit challenging for those who need to process information for a longer period of time or for those who have anxiety about how to respond to certain types of email. My guidance here is to and not overthink a response but still ensure your response is thoughtful. Tricky yes, but it can be done. 3) File – in some cases there are emails you need to save as reference. Make sure your file folders are well-organized so you can easily obtain past emails as needed.

2. Stay focused on your priorities and execute on them. If you feel pulled in too many directions, it may mean one of the following: a) you are taking on too much b) you are suffering from people pleasing syndrome c) you are having control issues and need to delegate more. On a weekly or even a daily basis, list the top priorities that need your attention and then take action.

3. Set firm boundaries for when you work. After finding myself feeling a bit burned out and needing to recharge my batteries more during non-working hours, I decide to set limits on when I work. This meant I had to set boundaries on when I checked work email, since there always seems to be a steady stream of incoming messages. For me, I try to refrain from checking email before 8AM and after 8PM and do my best to stay off email during the weekends. Also, I no longer have work email on my mobile phone. After making these changes, I feel more at peace instead of constantly having my energy pulled outward by demands of work.

4. Let go of what is out of your control. Often we are stressed out about work because we are worrying about things that are out of our control. We become upset because a situation didn't turn out the way we wanted or maybe someone didn't behave the way we expected them to. When we give our best at work but let go of expectations, a new sense of freedom will overcome us. We will focus on what we can do in the present moment and will let go of what might happen in the future. When worry is no longer an intruder in our mental state, we have the opportunity to allow for creative insight and strong problem solving skills to emerge.

Stressful situations are often a result of how we view them. If we can have a detached and objective view of a situation, it won't pull us in and overwhelm us. How do we achieve this objective state? We learn how to have control over our emotions which prevents us from immediately reacting when a stressful or challenging situation comes our way.

5. Regularly engage in activities that bring you joy and relaxation. For me, having a daily mediation and yoga practice helps me stay centered and calm. I also have made it a point to try and "lighten" up my life after dealing with SS (Serious Syndrome). Whether this means riding a moped with the wind whipping through my hair, watching funny movies, or just romping through nature, I have found it's imperative I have down time in my life where I can just be. No pressure from the outside world. No "To Do" lists ruling my life. Nothing to worry about except for just immersing myself in the present moment.

If we allow ourselves to fully recharge our batteries outside of work, we will be that more focused and productive when we are actually at work. Have fun. Explore. Allow your mind to wander. Take a break from one of your many electronic devices. Your mind and body will thank you.

Colleen Canney (colleencanney.com) is a Career and Spiritual Leadership Coach with clients around the world. Colleen brings a well-rounded background that includes an MBA and over ten years' experience working as a Human Resources professional in both the private and non-private sectors.

Lessons Learned from the Food Service Industry

By LINDA POURMASSINA, MD (Seattle, Washington) 18 February 2013

She sat in her crisp, white coat, probably not much older than I am now, leaning back with all of the assurance of someone who recently completed a cardiology fellowship, newly hired by the academic medical center to which I was applying for residency. One of the first of many interviews for me, the conversation was anything but smooth. She clearly wasn't sold on me. To remain genuine and avoid canned responses, I never bothered to research popular interview questions. Unfortunately, that also explains why I fumbled a little bit when answering "What three people who are not alive would you like to meet?"

I had just about given up on getting a good review from my interviewer, especially considering that she had already met some of my brilliant classmates whose parents worked for the same institution. But she had one more question for me. "So," she said, twisting her chair to the left with her arms crossed, looking at me a little sideways. "What makes you think you would make a good doctor? What have you done in the past that makes you think you would be a good physician?"

My answer was ready...and not because it was rehearsed. It wasn't the volunteering in nursing homes and Habitat for Humanity. It wasn't the good grades. It wasn't even because I was a caregiver at one point or because I had spent countless hours in labs.

"Waitressing, actually," I said this without hesitation and with an even tone. "I learned a lot by interacting and talking with customers." I knew I was taking a chance with this seemingly unsophisticated response, but I didn't seem to have much to lose at this point.

"You know," she said, looking surprised, suddenly animated, and mildly... exasperated? She turned to face me square on now. "My best friend keeps telling me the same thing. I don't get it, but she keeps telling me that it's true."

And then the ambience changed.

***

This having been my — paraphrased — experience years ago, I could not ignore a recent article entitled: "Do Starbucks Employees Have More Intelligence than Your Physician?"

The short answer is: Yes... and No, of course.

Articles like this paint a sharp caricature of the emotionally "unintelligent" physician. Here, Dr. Peter Ubel points out that Starbucks employees "undergo rigorous training in how to recognize and respond to customer needs," and he describes the Starbucks solution for dealing with unpleasant interactions, called the "Latte Method" (listening, acknowledging, taking action, thanking, and explaining). He contrasts this with the physician whose nose is

---

 Perhaps Dr. Ubel is on to something when he suggests that Starbucks employees have more emotional intelligence than physicians.

---

buried in labs, insensitive to the emotional needs of his patient.

Needless to say, a barista's work and a physician's work are not quite the same. A negative interaction within a doctor-patient environment is less like one in a food service industry and probably more similar to one experienced, say, by an airline customer service representative and a customer who finds himself unexpectedly stranded after his flight is cancelled, trying to get home in time for his mother's funeral. (A free coffee rarely solves this sort of problem.) The intensity of emotions tends to be quite high, the variables are many, and there can be a certain level of uncertainty that is uncomfortable for both parties involved. AND, there are multiple other people waiting in line with other high-intensity needs. There are certainly some doctors who seem oblivious to the emotional state of their patients. But there may be other factors, as well. For example, a burned out physician will find it difficult to empathize, and physicians who are essentially running on hamster wheels may feel too pressed for time to address complaints effectively. That being said, I happen to like the "Latte Method" described in the Forbes piece, as it can be applied to various aspects of our personal lives and across different industries.

A lot more work should be done in early medical training to help future doctors acknowledge and effectively deal with the unpleasant interactions between doctor and patient. Out of training now for some years, I was interested to hear about a group called The Balint Group, which focuses on exploring the doctor-patient relationship. Our clinic, The Polyclinic, has a Balint Group, so I decided to join and explore this subject some more. In this group, the meeting begins with one physician presenting a recent difficult or uncomfortable interaction. The rest of the physicians then discuss it by exploring both sides: what it must be like to be the doctor and what it might be like to be the patient in the case. It is very non-judgmental and not meant to be a problem-solving session. While many times there is no one right answer, the mere act of thinking about and discussing this topic can help improve interactions during the regular workday. I would recommend The Balint Group to any physician with an interest in the doctor-patient interaction.

Perhaps Dr. Ubel is on to something when he suggests that Starbucks employees have more emotional intelligence than physicians. Until Google Glasses that help detect facial cues become available and universally accepted, doctors will have to rely on their own radars, which may be fine-tuned with some more training. While I am not sure I could survive the Starbucks pace at this point, I did sign up some time ago to be a volunteer server for a local culinary and job training and placement program called FareStart.

Who knows? I may come back a better doctor for it.

Dr. Linda Pourmassina (pulsus.wordpress.com) practices at The Polyclinic in Seattle and is also on Facebook and Twitter. Her blog "Pulsus" is written from an Internal Medicine physician's perspective, for physicians and nonphysicians alike, with reflections on a variety of topics, with focus on the social and cultural aspects of medicine.

Bucket List

By CARRIE ELLEN BRUMMER (Dubai, United Arab Emirates) 25 Aug 2011

I am a teacher who lives overseas. I have been to places I had at one point never even knew existed (Sri Lanka, for example) and met people who have opened my eyes. When I return to the United States I often hear people tell me they are jealous of my lifestyle and are impressed by the things I do. Yes, all of this feeds an ego I don't need and also reminds me of just how lucky I am to lead the life I do... the thing I don't understand is why those who really want a change in circumstance don't make different choices?

Yes, humans are creatures of habit but we are also creatures of great innovation and can have huge, open hearts. We like to discover, explore, and learn. But we don't always apply that to our everyday.

I was a teacher who knew she wanted to travel. I fell upon a job that gave me training in an international curriculum, the I.B. Most people see "living overseas" as a wealthy person's perk but here I am, a teacher, who recently had Christmas in Rome.

There are ways to make what you want happen. Do you want to travel? Find a job opportunity with your skill set overseas (there are websites like that, for example TIE Online for educators). Save up money and apply for a sabbatical from your job. Have you always wanted a garden but don't know where to begin? Go to a library or Barnes and Noble on your lunch break and pick up Gardening for Dummies. Have you always talked about trying out for a roller derby team? Dust off those roller skates and use them one night per week instead of your run.

My wish list changes as my life changes. It has included going to Petra (done), learning how to garden (not yet) and owning my own puppy (not yet). Some of my other wishes are: see the Aurora Borealis, visit Ankor Wat, speak another language, write a novel, work for myself, make my own jewelry...

My point is (hopefully you have noted it) you only need to start with something small to begin working towards your "what ifs." Save your coffee money to work towards that cruise you always wanted. Sign up for an evening class to learn how to knit. All it takes is a choice. You make choices each and every day. Many people make choices that include, "When things slow down..." or, "When I have more job security." Do you want to know you checked something off of your wish list or look back and wish you made different choices? I haven't heard anyone in retirement say they wish they worked more. The only thing I have ever heard are things like, "I wish I made more time for my family," or, "I guess I never will see the Pyramids." It is just plain depressing to hear about the wish list unfulfilled instead of happy reminiscing about a life fully lived.

Be empowered. You are the only person in your way.

Carrie Ellen Brummer (artistthink.com) is an artist, a teacher, and a dreamer. She has been teaching Visual Arts for 8 years to students who have enriched her life! Carrie is also a practicing artist who has had art exhibits in both the United States and Dubai.

Why We Need to Write

By NINA MUNTEANU (Lunenburg, Nova Scotia) 18 December 2011

Words are a form of action, capable of influencing change
— Ingrid Bengis

We're all writers here... But how many of us, when asked about what we do, respond with "I write" or "I'm writing a book" or "I write stories"? I know. It's complicated. It's so much easier to leave that part out of our busy and serious lives. Besides, what do you say when the inevitable question of "so, what have you published?" comes up? All too often in North America, if you are not yet published you aren't considered a writer. Until you're published, you and your writing aren't taken seriously. Even after I was published, my husband called my writing a hobby. He's my ex-husband now.

What my ex-husband failed to recognize, but you and I know in our hearts, is that we live to write and write to live. Writing is the breath and light of our soul and the well-spring of our very essence. Isaac Asimov said, "I write for the same reason I breathe — because if I didn't, I would die." That was every bit as true when he was unpublished as after he'd published a bazillion books. This is more than metaphoric truth; it is scientifically proven.

Expressive writing — whether in the form of journaling, blogging, writing letters, memoir or fiction — improves health. Over the past twenty years, a growing body of literature has shown beneficial effects of writing about traumatic, emotional and stressful events on physical and emotional health. In control experiments with college students, Pennebaker and Beall (1986) demonstrated that college students who wrote about their deepest thoughts and feelings for only 15 minutes over four consecutive days, experienced significant health benefits four months later.

Long term benefits of expressive writing include improved lung and liver function, reduced blood pressure, reduced depression, improved functioning memory, sporting performance and greater psychological well-being. The kind of writing that heals, however, must link the trauma or deep event with the emotions and feelings they generated. Simply writing as catharsis won't do.

Whether you publish or not, your writing is important and worthwhile. Take ownership of it, nurture it, and hold it sacred. Command respect from others and respect all writers in turn; don't let ignorance intimidate you to silence. My colleague, Louise DeSalvo wrote in her book, Writing as a Way of Healing:

"Many people I know who want to write but don't or who want to write more but say they can't find the time, have told me that taking the time to write seems, well, self-indulgent, self-involved, frivolous even. And that finding the time to write — even a diary, much less fiction or memoir or poetry — in their busy schedules is impossible. 'I'll write when I have the time,' they say ... What, though, if writing weren't such a luxury? What if writing were a

 Writing is the breath and light of our soul and the well-spring of our very essence.

simple, significant, yet necessary way to achieve spiritual, emotional, and psychic wholeness? To synthesize thought and feeling, to understand how feeling relates to events in our lives and vice versa? What if writing were as important and as basic a human function and as significant to maintaining and promoting our psychic and physical wellness as, say, exercise, healthful good, pure water, clean air, rest and repose, and some soul-satisfying practice?"

Of course, in our hearts we know this is true. DeSalvo adds of her long journey toward accepting writing in her life: "I didn't know that if you want to write, you must follow your desire to write ... I didn't know that you could write simply to take care of yourself, even if you have no desire to publish your work. I didn't know that if you want to become a writer, eventually you'll learn through writing ... all you need to know about your craft ... I didn't know that if you want to write and don't, because you don't feel worthy enough or able enough, not writing will eventually begin to erase who you are."

Writing, like any form of creativity, requires faith; in ourselves and in others. And that's scary. It's scary because it requires that we relinquish control. All the more reason to write. Resistance is a form of self-destruction, says Julia Cameron, author of The Artist's Way (1992). We resist to maintain some idea of control but instead we increase depression, anxiety, and confusion. Booth et al (1997) found that written disclosure significantly reduces physiological stress on the body caused by inhibition. We were born to create. Why do we demure and resist? Because, says Cameron, "we have bought the message of our culture ... [that] we are meant to be dutiful and then die. The truth is that we are meant to be bountiful and live."

Joseph Campbell wrote: "Follow your bliss and doors will open where there were no doors before." Cameron adds, "It is the inner commitment to be true to ourselves and follow our dreams that triggers the support of the universe. While we are ambivalent, the universe will seem to us also to be ambivalent and erratic."

Seize the muse and proclaim it proudly. I AM A WRITER.

Nina Munteanu (ninamunteanu.com) has written several novels, short stories, and essays published worldwide and translated into several languages. Nina teaches and coaches writing through her website. Her acclaimed "The Fiction Writer: Get Published, Write Now!" is currently the textbook for creative writing classes at several universities and schools in North America.

Creating Hopeful Futures for Youth

By MARILYN PRICE-MITCHELL, Ph.D. (Bainbridge Island, Washington)
27 May 2011

Do you ever wonder how children grow up to be fulfilled, happy, and engaged in life? While there are no easy answers, we do know that three things make a big difference. First, children need positive life experiences that engage them in meaningful activities. Second, they need adults who help them believe in themselves. And last, they need families, schools, and communities who model and instill positive values.

I recently completed a research study with young people who had developed a passion for social and environmental causes. They saw a world beyond themselves — and wanted to make a difference. They were infused with hope and understood that even small acts of kindness had the potential to help others. They also had three things in common: meaningful life experiences, supportive adults, and positive values. Let's look briefly at these three powerful aspects of positive youth development.

Meaningful Life Experiences

Whether kids grow up in high or low-income households, children need positive experiences outside of classrooms and homework that bring meaning to their lives. Whether this is community service, sports, music, art, or other activities, it is important that children choose these activities for themselves.

Children learn best when life experiences have a degree of challenge. That is, activities must present opportunities for kids to overcome obstacles in order to succeed. Teens admit the more they are challenged in the real world, learn to get along with others, and practice solving problems, the more skills they learn to succeed in life.

Reflecting on her community service experiences, Mariah, age 19, said, "Coming from a small, homogeneous and affluent community, having the opportunity to interact with others from different backgrounds and social histories has allowed me to see just how fortunate I am, and to never take what my life has offered me for granted."

Supportive Adults

The well-known phase "it takes a village to raise a child" has been demonstrated over and over again through empirical research. Beyond good parenting, kids need other adults to support their development. In fact, grandparents, aunts, uncles, educators, clergy, coaches, and others who are involved in a child's life play an extremely vital role. They help children believe in themselves. Particularly in adolescence, youth need supportive adults to help in the process of discovering their unique identities, separate from their parents.

When you find yourself in the presence of teenagers who are not your own, you have an opportunity to listen without judgment, encourage, and get to know them as individuals, separate from their academic achievements. Showing a genuine interest in who they are rather than what they have achieved is how adolescents gain confidence in themselves.

Speaking of how her high school mentor helped her succeed, Danielle, age 19, said it well: "He wouldn't try to tell me what to do. He would instead just be thoughtful and quiet and then he would remind me who I was. He showed that he had faith in me and he knew that I would make a good choice."

Positive Values

Children who grow to be engaged, successful adults are instilled with positive values from a young age. Most children learn values from their families. But they also learn them at school, church, sports, and other after-school programs through the efforts of many adults. Positive values, including curiosity, love of learning, integrity, kindness, fairness, teamwork, humility, and gratitude are not ingrained in children by chance.

Not only do we model these values to the children in our lives but it's important to identify and discuss them with kids from childhood through adolescence. One way to develop these strengths is to praise kids when they act in kind, fair, or compassionate ways. By making praise more specific, we communicate appreciation for children's internal strengths, not just for what they achieve in school.

Speaking of how parents influenced her values, Grace, age 21, said, "I followed my own path for civic duty, but I looked to the strong examples that my parents set throughout their daily lives in order to stay true to the spirit of service and to not operate solely through a personal agenda of advancement."

Marilyn Price-Mitchell (rootsofaction.com) is a developmental psychologist, educator, researcher, and writer with a passion for learning how today's youth grow into healthy, successful, and engaged adults. She synthesizes multidisciplinary research in psychology, education, sociology, child & adolescent development, social psychology, and neurobiology to bring trusted, evidence-based research to parents, teachers, mentors, coaches, and all those who support kids.

Choice not Chance

By KAARINA DILLABOUGH (Amaranth, Ontario) 20 September 2011

I have spent most of my adult life choosing: the path less trodden, the people in need of inspiration and support, the places in my mind and soul that beckoned and the profession that has given me so much reward.

When I hear people say, "I have no choice", I want to rush to their side and help them to realize: EVERYTHING is choice. As the saying goes: "Choice, not chance, determines your destiny."

When people ask me, "What do you do?" I respond: "What do you need done?" Because if I can't help them, I'm quite confident I can find someone who can.

But people like labels, so I say: "I'm a coach, mentor and muse. *I'm the pat on the back, kick in the shins, neutral objective ally and accountability partner who's in your corner and on your team, always helping you to become the best you can be.*"

When we stop playing the blame game, and accept responsibility for our choices, decisions and actions, that's when true growth happens. But growth isn't always easy. That's why it's easier to blame external circumstances for our problems, rather than accepting and owning them as our own.

I lead a blessed life. YOU lead a blessed life. There might be times that you've lost sight of that. I'm here to remind you…to help you…to guide you.

My intention is to remind you of the power of your thoughts, and how those thoughts shape your reality, and influence each and every choice you make. Even to "not choose" is to choose.

When you accept and realize that you are the driver of your destiny, and not just a passenger on life's ride, you will begin to see possibilities that were always there: you just weren't seeing them. You will gain a sense of empowerment and pride that will propel you towards any goal you set. And we will talk about setting goals. Believing them. Achieving them.

I will bring a smorgasbord of information to your table, and I will ask you to heed the words of my own mentor, Jack Donahue, who said: "Take what I say and chew it around. If you don't like it, spit it out. But at least chew it around for a while."

And the information will be actionable. As a former Olympic level athletic coach, I know the power of visualization. But visualization alone won't cut it. You will need to TAKE ACTION. The stories I will share will help you to first: decide. Then: do.

I have been an entrepreneur all my life, and it's been a life of the highest highs and lowest lows. I know first-hand what it feels like to be handed defeat on a silver platter. I know what it's like when the people you thought were your friends and allies are nowhere to be found when the going gets tough. I've created three companies from scratch, one of which I had to close after two and a half years of painful, groundless litigation. I know what it's like to see all that you've built; crushed.

But more importantly, I know what it's like to wake every day and realize: I'm creating the life I'm living. YOU are creating the life YOU'RE living. Let's journey together.

Kaarina Dillabough (kaarinadillabough.com) is a business consultant, coach and strategist. Her high-voltage energy, passion, expertise and experience inspire those she works with to reach beyond their grasp, to attain great things in business and in life. As a former Olympic level coach, Kaarina applies the same approach to individuals as she did with athletes: lighting the fire within to help people see their true potential. A popular speaker, Kaarina has an engaging storytelling style that never fails to inform, educate and entertain. Her content is always fresh and full of value, as she combines a wealth of leading-edge information with her own unique point of view.

Making Life and Work a Work of Art

By LINDA NAIMAN, (Vancouver, British Columbia) 13 May 2011

Mihaly Csikszentmihalyi, best known for his research on creativity, and his book Flow: The Psychology of Optimal Experience, says "How we choose what we do, and how we approach it...will determine whether the sum of our days adds up to a formless blur, or to something resembling a work of art."

Sometimes it seems that my life is a formless blur, especially when I lose my focus in a flurry of chaotic busyness, and I'm plagued by a steady stream of necessary yet un-enjoyable tasks that don't seem to get finished, stalling creative projects that would give me a lot more satisfaction...if only I could get to them. This isn't art; this is a tedious mess! And worse, I've lost my flow!

Art for me is soul food. Art-making is meditation in action. It nourishes my craving for beauty, clarity and harmony. By beauty, I mean aesthetics, that is, the beauty of meaning-making, when all the parts come together to create a whole, or when clues are combined to solve a mystery. It's about finding elegant solutions to problems we face. It's the profound simplicity we discover on the other side of complexity, once we've dug through our messes.

Artistry can be defined as having mastered a skill sufficiently enough that you don't have to think about it. Artistry is the bridge between concept and craft. Once you have mastered a skill you can transcend technicalities and focus on creating, inventing and innovating.

Artists constantly work their craft by developing their skills. In order to take on more challenge and stay in the flow, you may need to learn new skills. Mastery is what separates the virtuoso from the technician, in music, dance, theatre and art.

What is your art? Is it leadership? Parenting? Teaching? Entertaining? Artistic qualities such as seeing with new eyes, sensing and perceiving, mastery, elegance, finding beauty, meaning, balance, harmony, emotional truth, melody, rhythm, and composition, can be applied to all aspects of our lives. Reflect on each of these qualities and ask yourself which ones are present in your life and which ones are missing.

Don't get caught up in creating a masterpiece. Focus instead on developing your craft in whatever art form appeals to you. Slow down and become absorbed in the process. When you relax and enter that place of flow, you will notice your mind quiet down, and creative imagination start to bubble up.

When I coach people undergoing a transition in their lives, I encourage them to be imaginative, and to question assumptions about their challenges. Each one of us has unique talents, and creative means of expression. If you could design your future, what would it look like? How would you compose the different elements? In what ways can you bring artistry to your life and work? Rather than focusing on problems, we focus on possibilities, and finding artful solutions.

Linda Naiman (creativityatwork.com) is founder of Creativity at Work and co-author of Orchestrating Collaboration at Work. She is a pioneer in arts-based learning for business and provides creativity and innovation expertise to clients in North America, Europe and Asia. She also coaches executives, entrepreneurs and change agents on leadership, creativity, innovation and career advancement. Linda has been featured in The Vancouver Sun, The New Zealand Herald, The Globe and Mail, and Canadian Business Magazine.

What Will You Do in Retirement?

By ANN HARRISON (Manchester, United Kingdom) 05 October 2011

Retirement can, on average, free up between 2,000 and 3,000 hours per year. That's after you add in the time you spend commuting, thinking about and working on work-related tasks at home and physically getting ready for work each day.

So, how will you fill those 2,000 to 3,000 hours once you retire?

Will you spend more time sleeping?

If you've spent the whole of your working life feeling sleep-deprived because you just didn't have enough time to do everything on your to-do list, you might be looking forward to those long lie-ins once you retire.

And, of course, many people who are, by nature, 'night owls' have been forced into becoming 'larks' because of the demands of their jobs and parenthood. If that sounds like you, when you no longer have to be up and at 'em at the crack of dawn every day, you may find yourself reverting to the night owl you always were at heart.

On the other hand, you might be determined to make the most of all the time you've freed up and adopt an 'I'll sleep when I'm dead' attitude.

Will you still work?

Do you intend to retire completely or are you one of the estimated 7 out of 10 people who wants or needs to carry on working (in some capacity) once you reach the traditional age for retirement?

There's a lot of evidence to suggest that the people who have the most successful retirements are the ones who keep themselves active and engaged.

There's also a lot of evidence that many people nowadays don't actually want to retire at all. They just want to do something else and they want to do it on their own terms — for example, they want to be able to choose when they work and for how long. Or they want to do something completely different — such as voluntary work in a different field to the one in which they made their living. So the big question is: Do you want, need or feel that it would be beneficial to continue to work after you 'officially' retire?

Will you spend more time with your family?

How much time do you want to spend with family members after you retire? Some questions to think about in this area include:

What expectations do your partner, your children, your grandchildren and your elderly parents have about your retirement? Do your expectations and theirs blend together? Will someone be expecting more of you than you are prepared to give? Does someone have their eye on you as a potential babysitter or caregiver and what effect will this have on your own plans for your retirement?

Will you spend more time on your hobbies?

If you're the type of person who's never had a problem filling their spare time, you probably already have a satisfying blend of hobbies, interests and pastimes to look forward to when you retire.

If you've never had time for hobbies, you might need to rethink that perspective now. Ask yourself: Are my current hobbies, interests and activities going to be enough to sustain me and keep me interested and connected in retirement? If not, spend some time investigating some potential new hobbies and interests. Try them on to see if they fit. And don't forget to revisit some of those things that you used to enjoy but which got crowded out of your life by the pressures of work and bringing up a family.

Will you spend more time on community or voluntary activities?

Many retirees like to do voluntary work as a way of giving back to society and providing themselves with a sense of fulfillment and a feeling of being useful. How much time (if any) would you like to devote to voluntary or community activities in your retirement? Which voluntary activities do you feel naturally drawn to? What voluntary activities are you aware of in your area/community? Which, if any, of these appeal to you? What's the next step?

Remember, you can take your time and try out various voluntary activities before committing yourself. Don't get stuck doing something you don't enjoy because you'd feel guilty if you gave it up.

Will you take more time for yourself?

Many people report that the best thing about being retired is that they can take the time to do all the pleasurable little things that they never had time to do when they were working. Things like reading the paper from cover to cover, having an extra cup of coffee in bed before they get up, or going to a movie matinee. What are the 'little things' that you're looking forward to doing? Make sure you don't get so busy in retirement that you don't have time to indulge in the little things that would bring you pleasure.

Once you get started, you'll probably find you have no problems filling those 2,000 hours. In fact, you'll probably wonder how you found time to work at all!

Ann Harrison (contemporaryretirement.typepad.com) is a Retirement Options™ trained retirement coach and Too Young To Retire™ facilitator. She is also a writer, blogger and creator of information products; she retired from her job in education management at the ripe old age of forty-three. She is the author of ebooks, "The Retirement Detox Programme: 40 days to get your retirement back on track" and 'Thought Provokers: Questions you need to ask yourself BEFORE you retire".

What Are You Packing on Life's Journey?

By KAARINA DILLABOUGH (Amaranth, Ontario) 13 January 2012

I was looking at my antique suitcases the other day. They aren't mine. Well, now they are. But they once belonged to someone from another time and place...a time and place far removed from today.

As I stood admiring the suitcases' frayed leather straps, now-fading stickers from far-flung places, intricate brass corners and fancy lock-and-key closure, I imagined what the original owner might have packed inside...for what trip...for what purpose.

Did they take a minimalist approach, packing only the essentials? Or did they cram every conceivable "might need this" piece of clothing and paraphernalia inside, 'til the suitcase required a feat of strength, simply to close the latches?

Were the items neatly folded and arranged, making maximum use of the space while maintaining minimal disruption to the contents en route? Or were things simply thrown willy-nilly into the case, with much grunting and groaning about how things just didn't fit...there was just too much to fit into this small space... and there was just no time to re-pack it, or pack it properly in the first place.

Each day is like a suitcase. It has a limited amount of space and time. And that space and time can be crammed full of "stuff", or it can be filled with the essentials.

How heavy is your suitcase? Are you struggling under its weight, or moving along with ease? If you've packed too much into your suitcase...your day...then it's inevitable that you will feel weary, frustrated and exhausted as you haul your day's work, like an anchor behind you, only to fall into bed depleted...to start packing the next day full to the brim.

Lighten your load. Remove the things you do not need. Pack

the important things. Include the beautiful things. Place the productive things into the suitcase that is your day.

And if you've tried to make your day one of multiple suitcases…stop. Cast a critical eye on all that you're carrying.

I often use imagery when working with clients, and the suitcase image is one that seems to fit quite well when someone is feeling overburdened, overwhelmed and just plain tired. This is how it goes:

Imagine yourself on a beautiful beach. You've arrived from your home, laden down with suitcases, full of things you think you'll need. You've over-packed, and you know it. Your neck is stiff. Your arms are tired. Your back is aching. The weight of all that you're carrying feels like the weight of the world.

Now picture yourself taking a few steps along the beach, placing one suitcase down. This allows you to stand a little straighter and walk a little lighter.

 Each day is like a suitcase. It has a limited amount of space and time.

Take a few more steps and place another suitcase down. Whew. That feels good. You smile. You actually take in the scenery around you for the first time. It's really beautiful.

A few more steps and another suitcase left on the beach. You now feel liberated, expansive, light and full of energy. You continue until all the suitcases are lined up behind you along the beach, and you have moved beyond them. You look back, seeing the burdens you've been carrying. You laugh, realizing that most of what you were carrying was unnecessary, and served only to burden you, not lighten your load. You resolve to pack lighter now.

For me, that means doing the important things each and every day, and not permitting time-wasting, energy-sucking people or things to take priority over the important stuff. It means putting the big rocks in first. What are your big rocks?

What baggage can you leave behind on the beach today?

Kaarina Dillabough (kaarinadillabough.com) *is a business consultant, coach and strategist. Her high-voltage energy, passion, expertise and experience inspire those she works with to reach beyond their grasp, to attain great things in business and in life. As a former Olympic level coach, Kaarina applies the same approach to individuals as she did with athletes: lighting the fire within to help people see their true potential. A popular speaker, Kaarina has an engaging storytelling style that never fails to inform, educate and entertain. Her content is always fresh and full of value, as she combines a wealth of leading-edge information with her own unique point of view.*

Four Occasions When It's Best to Keep Quiet

By GWYN TEATRO *(Vancouver, British Columbia) 31 January 2013*

Will Rogers once said, "Never miss a good chance to shut up".

I think he has a point. Rarely though, do we consider that effective communication also means keeping quiet. And yet, nothing can be more effective in reaching understanding than a well-placed pause, a time when we step back and listen, not only to others but also to ourselves.

It's a discipline I think all leaders need to develop. But first we have to be able to readily recognize when we are talking too much and listening too little and, as a result, eroding the depth and importance of our conversations.

So when might that happen to you? Well, I can think of a few occasions when it might and here they are:

When you're angry ~ (Subtext: I'm mad so I'm going to vent all over you so that I can feel better).

Anger sometimes compels us to put the mouth in gear before the brain has had time to process what's going on. And that can make a bad situation worse.

Being on the receiving end of someone's flare-up is also very off-putting and a sure-fire way of shutting down lines of communication altogether.

When you're tempted to say any old thing to fill a void ~ (Subtext: I'm uncomfortable so I'm going to say something because **somebody** has to!)

Silence can be cringe-worthy. For instance, in a meeting you put an idea up for discussion; you ask for some thoughts … and nothing happens. But, if you start talking just to relieve the tension, chances are, you are missing an opportunity to hear from someone who simply needs a little time to process the information before sharing his or her opinion. So, tolerating pauses, pregnant or otherwise, could be a very positive discipline to develop.

When you're convinced of your 'rightness' ~ (Subtext: I'm right and I'm going to keep on talking until you agree with me).

Sometimes we can fall in love with our own ideas so much that we make no space for the possibility that we may be wrong. Clinging to a position and arguing its virtues can be great fun but if we are not willing to listen to others' perspectives and soften the edges of our views in the face of new information, we become a roadblock to progress.

When you realize you don't really know what you're talking about ~ (Subtext: I'm lost but I'll look like a fool if I stop talking now.)

Every once in a while I will embark on a line of conversation… and then lose the thread. Instead of stopping to get re-focused, I will keep talking in the hope that eventually, I'll get to the point. I don't think I'm particularly unique in this. When it happens, it's embarrassing but frankly so is taking people on a meander that you didn't intend. As for me, I find it helps to simply stop, mid-ramble, and admit that I have no idea where I was going. We all have a laugh and get to move on to something more productive.

There is of course a common theme running through the occasions I've described. Each of them is a self-indulgent response. In communication, as in leadership, self-indulgence will get in the way of success every time.

That's what I think anyway. What do you think?

Are You Living in the Middle of the Hunger Games?

By IAN LAWTON (Grand Haven, Michigan) 06 March 2013

Do you ever feel like you're living in the middle of Hunger Games; you know, like the world is a battle for survival with everyone out to protect their own at any cost?

Not everyone of course. You meet all sorts of people and situations. Some people shock me with kindness. The unforgiving nastiness of others makes my head hurt.

Joan of Arc said,

Every man gives his life for what he believes ... one life is all we have to live and we live it according to what we believe.

I wish this were true. More often it seems that the way people act bears little relationship to what they say they believe. I've seen the same proportion of kindness and nastiness in churches as out of churches, and the same blend of generosity and territorialism inside positive inspiration circles as out. It makes me wonder what's the point of so-called beliefs if you don't see any fruits.

I guess the trick is to focus on the kindness, make sure I live my own life with integrity, and let the rest take care of itself.

I like the way Mary Oliver describes it,

Every day I see or hear something that more or less kills me with delight, that leaves me like a needle in the haystack of light.

Focus on the people and situations that more or less kill me with delight, even if kindness feels like a needle in a haystack of cruelty.

Recently I've been reading Hunger Games with my son. We're half way through book two, and I'm pretty well riveted. If you don't know the story, it centers around two kids, Katniss and Peeta, who are drawn in the lottery as Hunger Games' contestants. They come from one of the outlying districts. Each district sends two kids into a battle to the death, all for the entertainment (and social control) of the oppressive Capitol.

The night before they head in to battle, Peeta tries to explain to Katniss how he wants to die, but he can't quite find the words. Peeta says, "'I don't know how to say it exactly. Only... I want to die as myself. Does that make any sense?'" It doesn't make sense to Katniss, at least not yet. She wonders, "How could he die as anyone but himself?" Peeta explains: "'I don't want them to change me in there. Turn me into some kind of monster that I'm not.... I keep wishing I could think of a way to show the Capitol they don't own me. That I'm more than just a piece in their Games.'"

Eventually, Katniss "gets" it. She decides to do it on her own terms.

That's the point. Live or die, but do it on your own terms, and let those terms be an expression of who you really are and not who you think others need you to be, or society tries to force you to be. I choose not to buy into the nastiness of anyone else. In so doing, no matter the outcome of the game called life, I can't lose.

We crave heroes, the Peetas and Katnisses of the world, who model this sort of integrity in the heat of battle.

Maybe more to the point, we want to BE those people in the way we live our lives. And it IS in our control to make that choice. Most of us won't do it in grand, public battles of life and death. It more often happens through small, even unnoticed acts of kindness. As David Foster Wallace said,

The really important kind of freedom involves attention, and awareness, and discipline, and effort, and being able truly to care about other people and to sacrifice for them, over and over, in myriad petty little unsexy ways, every day.

Millions Saw the Apple Fall, but Newton Asked Why

By CONNIE DENESIUK (Summerland, British Columbia) 10 July 2011

I don't know the year or occasion when American statesman Bernard Baruch first declared: *Millions saw the apple fall, but Newton asked why.* What I do know for sure, though, is its meaning and importance.

Curiosity.

It didn't kill the cat (as the proverb suggests) but spurred many on to greatness. Curiosity is that rare kind of inquisitive interest and hunger for explanations that seems to go hand in hand with genius.

Dr. Ken Tapping is that kind of person. He works as an astronomer with the National Research Council at the Dominion Radio Astrophysical Observatory near White Lake (in southern Okanagan, BC). Many may know him as the "Star Gazer" for his national newspaper column "Stargazing". He has also represented Canadian interests as a delegate to the International Telecommunications Union in Geneva, and has been awarded the National Research Council's Outstanding Achievement award.

With the extensive research that Dr. Tapping has conducted on our solar system and beyond, I was somewhat surprised to find that his curiosity extends far beyond his established field of expertise. For example, he raises cacti and ant colonies. He loves art and music and is completing a book on local geology titled, *Exploring the Last Ice Age in the Southern Okanagan*.

Dr. Tapping believes that curiosity is an important component in the way humanity adapts and moves forward.

"A certain fraction of the population maintains that natural childhood curiosity," he said. "It is curiosity that drives and advances us, and urges us on in finding new frontiers. Curiosity keeps us wondering what is under that rock, what is behind that hill, and plays an important role in our society."

He acknowledges that everyone possesses curiosity to some extent but there are some people who have it real bad.

"They are," he said, "the sort of people who find the edge of the world by falling off it!"

I probed further. I asked him (in my best Barbara Walters style) of three things he was most curious about. Here's what he said:

1. How do clouds work?

2. Chaos. I would like to understand "chaos" in more detail, because one is starting to see how a very small nudge in nature can create huge changes. I think understanding the theory of chaos would be absolutely fantastic.

3. I'd like to watch ants for a year or two. Ants, in their own way, have a society unlike ours and it seems to work. Ants have a lot of the same vices as people. For example, they will stop working if no one is looking and they have a soft spot for alcohol. I'd like to go to the garden and just watch them.

And, Dr. Tapping's advice to the curious?

Stay curious. Ask questions, and then be prepared to learn. If you see an unusual fruit on a tree and say to yourself 'that's an unusual fruit', then pick one. Cut it in half, and wonder why it's like that. Be prepared to try to find an answer. Curiosity is very active. Don't be afraid to ask questions.

Or, stated another way, "Millions saw the apple fall, but Newton asked why".

Connie Denesiuk has a long history of community involvement in the Okanagan region of British Columbia. She brings a blend of common sense and optimism to her work. In addition to serving as a long time school trustee and as President of BC School Trustees Association, Connie and her husband Bob have been partners in their construction business for more than thirty years.

Seven Habits of Highly Creative People

By LINDA NAIMAN, (Vancouver, British Columbia) 22 June 2011

Creativity is the act of turning new and imaginative ideas into reality. Creativity involves two processes: thinking, and then producing. Innovation is the production or implementation of an idea. If you have ideas, but don't act on them, you are imaginative but not creative. Make a habit of these seven practices, and you will be highly creative in your field.

1. Prepare the ground

"In creating, the only hard thing's to begin; A grass-blade's no easier to make than an oak." —James Russell Lowell

Creativity requires an absorbed mind, a relaxed state of focus and attention. Give yourself the time and space you need to get completely absorbed in the zone of creativity and inspiration. Let the desire to create come from the pure pleasure of creative expression. If you worry about being perfect, you may never begin.

2. Plant seeds for creativity

"We are what we think. All that we are arises with our thoughts. With our thoughts we create the world." —The Buddha

We amplify what we think about most. Put your attention on what you want to create, not on complaints. Set an intention to produce the results you desire.

3. Live in the question

"Be patient towards all that is unsolved in your heart. And try to love the questions themselves." —Rainer Maria Rilke

It's been said that at the age of 5, children ask 120 questions a day, at age 6 they ask only 60 questions a day, and at the age of 40, adults ask 4 questions a day. We adults need to embrace "beginner's mind," and ask questions, instead of trying to find immediate answers. Pay attention to questions other people ask, especially those from artists, scientists, and thought leaders. Collect questions you find compelling.

4. Feed your brain

"If you stuff yourself full of poems, essays, plays, stories, novels, films, comic strips, magazines, music, you automatically explode every morning like old faithful. I have never had a dry spell in my life, mainly because I feed myself well, to the point of bursting." — Ray Bradbury

Be curious and follow your nose. Get interested in something and it will later provide you with a goldmine of ideas if you learn to make connections between people, places and things that would not ordinarily be connected. Combining ideas, and making connections are key practices of creativity employed by artists, designers, and scientists.

5. Experiment & explore

"I make more mistakes than anyone else I know, and sooner or later, I patent most of them." — Thomas Edison

Edison was a both a prolific inventor and innovator, producing over 1,093 patents. He was also a master at learning from failed experiments. When he died in 1931 he left behind 3,500 notebooks containing details of his ideas and thoughts. If you follow your curiosity, experiment with ideas, and learn from your mistakes, the quality of your creativity will vastly improve.

6. Replenish your creative stock

"As artists, we must learn to be self-nourishing." — Julia Cameron

Joni Mitchell describes her replenishing process as field rotation. When she needs a break, she switches form singing and songwriting to painting.

7. The secret to liberating your creativity

There is no magic bullet that will liberate your creativity, but it can be helpful to remember how you played as a child. What absorbed you to the extent that you lost track of time? Your child's play provides the clue to your creativity, your talents and your passion. What connections can you make from lessons you have learned at play, that you can apply to your work?

Creativity takes on many forms in business, art, design, education and science. When we express our creativity in these domains, we have the ability to make life and work a work of art.

Linda Naiman (creativityatwork.com) *is founder of Creativity at Work and co-author of Orchestrating Collaboration at Work. She is a pioneer in arts-based learning for business and provides creativity and innovation expertise to clients in North America, Europe and Asia. She also coaches executives, entrepreneurs and change agents on leadership, creativity, innovation and career advancement. Linda has been featured in The Vancouver Sun, The New Zealand Herald, The Globe and Mail, and Canadian Business Magazine.*

How to Accept Rejection

By NINA MUNTEANU (Lunenburg, Nova Scotia) 21 May 2013

We've all suffered rejection and disappointment. Perhaps that job you coveted or someone you loved who might have even led you on before dropping you. It hurts. But you move on. And it does get better. It does, trust me.

Being a published writer involves accepting rejection. Think of rejection as an integral part of your road to success. If you have never been rejected then you haven't really tried, have you? There are several ways that you can gain a good perspective on your rejection letters and even make them work to your advantage.

Adopt a Healthy Perspective

One way is to adopt a realistic, objective and healthy view-point on your story's rejection:

View selling manuscripts as a "cold call" business: When you view it this way, you will treat it that way. Until you establish a relationship with your market, selling becomes a numbers game. The more you send, the more likely you are to get a hit. It's all in the statistics.

View rejections as an opportunity. Rejections can provide you with the opportunity to learn and re-evaluate, usually of appropriate market and publisher subjectivity rather than writing quality.

View rejections as the beginning of a relationship. Not all rejections are final; in fact most aren't. Most rejections by a publisher or magazine editor stem from story redundancy, lack of space or editorial requirements. Many rejection letters will reflect this (e.g., "Thanks, but this isn't a match for us…do try us again." They mean it. It just means that the story wasn't right—they may have run something too similar to it already or it didn't fit with the other pieces or theme or whatever.)

View rejections as part of your success journey. Rejection is a given in the writing business and a necessary aspect of your journey as a soon-to-be and published writer (you don't stop getting rejections once you're published!). Often a story may be considered "before its time"; too different, a risk and is therefore harder to place. This is often why a book that was rejected so many times becomes a great hit once it is published. The very quality that made it hard for a publisher to accept made it a success with the readership: its refreshing yet topical originality.

View rejections as your first step to success. Take heart in the fact that you reached this stage in your writing career. Getting that first rejection in the mail is a great affirmation that you have taken that first significant step to becoming a serious writer. It means that you've completed a work and had the courage to enter it into the world.

Acceptance begins with rejection.

Make Rejection Work for You

You can maintain a more objective view on your rejections by keeping an objective view on your submissions. This can be accomplished by submitting a lot and submitting often. Treat your submissions — and rejections — like a business. The best way to do this is to submit lots of stories and to keep submitting them. The critical part of this process is to always have a contingency ready for each story submitted: once a story is returned, you have a place to send it already. Most professional writers will recommend that you do not revise the story before resending it out. This is because many rejections occur not on account of poor writing, but because of poor or unlucky marketing.

Remember that You're in Great Company

Virtually every writer of merit who has published has had their work rejected several times. Beatrix Potter's The Tale of Peter Rabbit was turned down so many times that she initially self-published. Irving Stone's Lust for Life was rejected sixteen times before a publisher finally picked it up and sold about twenty-five million copies. Not bad for a story that was passed off as "a long, dull novel about an artist." Jonathan Livingston Seagull was turned down twenty-three times and Dune twenty-one times.

Nina Munteanu (ninamunteanu.com) has written several novels, short stories, and essays published worldwide and translated into several languages. Nina teaches and coaches writing through her website. Her acclaimed "The Fiction Writer: Get Published, Write Now!" is currently the textbook for creative writing classes at several universities and schools in North America.

Keeping an Open Mind

By ZEE GORMAN (San Francisco, California) 23 August 2011

With age comes experience. And with experience we so often become close-minded.

Last year I told my professional friend about some of the challenges at work. In response, he recommended a book. It was about communication. Having been a corporate manager for over ten years, I have attended countless management, leadership and communication classes, conferences and seminars. They teach me how to listen, how to negotiate, how to address the elephant in the room, how to manage employee performance, how to resolve conflicts – you name it. All of these classes have been helpful but nothing is transformational. At the end of the day, I go about my work being my professional self. I draw from my experience and I have been quite successful – not outstandingly successful but who doesn't have some challenges?

So of course when he told me to buy this book, I dismissed it as, well, one of those things that sound good in theory.

Six months later I talked to him again and he asked if I had bought the book. Other than being a bit surprised that he still remembered, I felt guilty. I asked for his advice and then turned around and ignored it. Out of guilt I searched my Inbox for the Amazon link he sent me and ordered the book.

When the book arrived, I flipped through it without really reading it and then put it back down. He said to buy it, but he never said to read it, right? I chuckled to myself. Whatever advice the book would offer, I was sure I had read it somewhere, heard it in a speech and chances are, I had even practiced it. Heck I could write a book about communication. How would this help me with my real world problems?

The inevitable came when I talked to my friend again. He asked if I had read the book. I confessed I hadn't and I promised that I would.

That night after I brewed a cup of herbal tea and got comfortable in my pajamas, I took the book off my bookshelf. I shook my head at the unspectacular book cover and the cliché-sounding title and then turned to the first page. I skipped the acknowledgement, praises, foreword and what not and dove right into the meat – the first line of the first chapter.

It was a poem. I read the first few lines. The words grabbed me. I was surprised at first and then as I continued on with the content, I began to be drawn in. I had to put it down at midnight and go to bed because I had work the next day. But as soon as I had a break I picked up where I left off and continued reading it.

I finished the book within 24 hours. But I felt I wanted more of the same. I searched online for more information about the author and found a non-profit organization that teaches the foundation of the communication skills as taught in this book. I went online, found the classes and immediately registered for the first class available in my area.

 That night after I brewed a cup of herbal tea and got comfortable in my pajamas, I took the book off my bookshelf.

I had so much fun (and learned so much) in my first class that I registered for another one. I just can't seem to get enough of this! It was such a transformational experience that I told my husband, my best friend and many of my peers about it.

Not surprisingly, they laughed it off or politely ignored me. I suddenly saw myself in them – someone who "has been there, done that and knows it all" and who no longer wants to learn. More importantly, we no longer want to change ourselves. We may be successful, may not be so successful, or we know our strengths and shortcomings, and our spouses' and colleagues' strengths and shortcomings to such an extent that we no longer feel the need to shake things up.

It is as my friend said: "My husband likes to complain. It's his thing. I have to let him. It works for us. I don't want to touch it." Surely complaining is not a good thing right? Weren't we taught not to complain when we were young? Since when did complaining become something acceptable? Obviously since we gave up changing, learning, and striving for a better self and therefore a better life!

Or it is as my husband said: "Oh it teaches you how to listen right? I know how to listen. I just choose not to sometimes." When we didn't do something when we were young, it is because we didn't know any better. But now we are old enough to know, we simply choose to not do them. We have come to accept who we are! That is a good thing. But on the other hand, it is a bad thing because we have given up the climb.

Yes, for the most part, this non-spectacular book written over thirty years ago teaches many of the same things that we learned in kindergarten. Perhaps if you read it, you may find nothing useful in it. But boy am I glad I read it! What it did for me no other communication classes have done. It transformed my thinking on things I thought I had answers for. It helped me navigate a difficult situation at work. It helped me build connection with my teenage daughter. It is now helping me every single day.

More importantly, this experience taught me that I don't have to accept how things are because I have been there done that and know it all. It taught me to keep an open eye for that rare gem around the corner that may transform my life for the better.

It taught me to put my experience on the side and keep an open mind.

Zee Gorman (zeegorman.blogspot.ca), born in South China during the Cultural Revolution (both her parents were exiled to the countryside for being 'intellectuals'), was raised within layers of political and cultural confines. Yet her love for literature gave wings to a life that would be completely different from that of her parents. She has written short stories, poems, and essays, and is mildly published in China. Her quest and thirst for more understanding of the Western cultures eventually led to her migration to the United States where she completed two Master's Degrees at Northern Arizona University. Today, Zee Gorman lives in Northern California with her husband and her daughter. By night she is a writer, an artist, a crafter... whatever she imagines herself to be and by day she has a career in IT management.

10 Steps to Learning How to Live Joyfully

By GAIL BRENNER (Santa Barbara, California) 09 October 2011

"I wish I could show you when you are lonely or in darkness the astonishing light of your own being." ~Hafiz of Persia

Are you moving too fast to enjoy life? Are you caught up in problems and struggles? Are you pressing forward on automatic, burning the candle at both ends?

This article is all about slowing down – and I'm writing it for myself as much as for anyone reading this. Because it's time to stop, be still, hop off the treadmill, and return to sanity.

It's so easy to slip away from being aware. Even with the best of intentions, before we know it, we find ourselves moving mindlessly through life. We go through the motions, taking care of obligations, inhabiting habit patterns, and meanwhile longing for a time when the to-do list is empty. Our minds are caught in mental whirlwinds while we are missing out on what is already here.

We feel separate, deadened, and half-alive.

Joyful living takes commitment. It asks us to be awake and aware in the moments of our lives. It invites us to stem the momentum of our habits so we can reclaim peace, appreciation, wonder, awe, presence.

Do you want to master the art of joyful living? Integrate these 10 steps in your life, and the seeds of joy will flourish endlessly.

1. Bring silence and stillness into your life

If we turn down the volume on all the noise in our lives, we discover the amazing fact that silence and stillness are already here. And when we intentionally allow ourselves to be still, we naturally open to a deep appreciation of the present moment. We become relaxed, grounded, and clear, and stress begins to melt away.

How can you bring silence into your life? When can you stop and be still?

2. Clean up

Someone recently told me she feels disgusted when she looks into her closet because of all the clutter. It's a shame because every moment of disgust is a moment empty of joy.

If there is anything you are procrastinating about, anything you can easily fix, anyone who drags you down, pay attention. Don't wait or settle for good enough. Carve out the time, figure out a solution, and clean it up. You are making the space for joy, peace, and happiness to illuminate your life.

3. Mind your own business

Do you want to be unhappy and frustrated? Then try controlling things you can't actually do anything about. Like other people or most situations or the past or future.

If you are caught in an emotional reaction, turn the mirror onto yourself. Let the story go, and see what is actually true in your direct experience. Bring compassion right into the places where it is needed most. Diligently work on the areas where you get stuck, and joy will naturally shine through you.

4. Give to others whatever you feel you are lacking

So many of us want attention, love, and understanding. We live in a state of lack, thinking that life can begin if only we get what we think we need.

Consider that you may not actually need what you think you need. It might just be an old story that has outworn its welcome.

Instead of living in lack, contemplate generosity. Give out to others what you want or need. Pull out the stops in offering attention, interest, and caring. Your sense of lack will be transformed into fullness. Believing you don't have enough becomes love overflowing.

5. Use your senses

Life is so abundant right before our very eyes. Slow down and take the time to see, hear, taste, touch, and smell. Eating an apple becomes a sensual delight, doing the dishes a symphony.

6. Recognize what is working

It is so easy to focus on problems and unhappy feelings. They grab our attention and won't let go like a dog feasting on a juicy bone.

Take stock of what is working in your life. Is your living situation a good one? Do you know people who you love and appreciate? Do you enjoy your daily runs or a good home-cooked meal? Simply look around you, and you may be surprised by the bounty that is already present.

7. Live in forgiveness

If a grudge is interfering with your joy of life, then it requires your loving attention. Don't let the minutes tick by while you live in self-righteousness or regret. Neutralize the stories from the past, and make the choice to live joyfully now.

Then live in amends. If you feel wronged by someone or you hurt another, deal with it. Don't let it fester. Make a lifestyle of living free from hurts and grudges. You will feel strong, clear, and empowered.

8. Learn from life experiences

Sometimes the road of life is a bumpy one. If you want to master joyful living, be open to learning from the challenges that life brings you. Be honest about what buttons get pushed and recognize when you have dropped into a hole that you can't seem to find your way out of.

Difficult life experiences are designed to show us the areas in our lives where we are not yet free. Use these situations well for your own liberation. You might have noticed that the teachings come until we understand the lesson. If there is a self-defeating pattern playing out in your life, slow it down so you can become conscious of what you are doing. Then make different, better choices with your eyes wide open.

9. Be pleasant

No matter what is going on in your life, show up in an open, good-natured way. No one likes a Negative Nancy. Stop complaining, and instead be patient, open, kind, and agreeable in your day-to-day life.

10. Move in the direction of joy

Every moment offers a choice.

Joy provides the perfect barometer for navigating through life. All you need to do is recognize what brings you joy, then follow it. Simple, right? Make room in your life for what is positive, light, and life-affirming. You will have mastered the art of joyful living.

Dr. Gail Brenner (aflourishinglife.com) is a blogger and psychologist with 20 years experience offering psychotherapy. She has worked with adults, elders, couples, families, and teenagers as well as people with pain and chronic medical problems. Her therapy involves helping people gain the insights they need to release mental and emotional patterns that distract from happiness, inner peace, and full creative expression.

Want to Make a Change in Your Life?

By ANN HARRISON (Manchester, United Kingdom) 05 November 2011

> *"A journey of a thousand miles must begin with the first step."*
> *- Lao Tzu*

When someone wants to make a change in their life — such as losing weight, getting fitter or eating healthier, they usually do something drastic. For example, they'll cut their calorie intake to 1000 a day and vow never to eat cakes, cookies or pizza ever again. Or they'll make a decision that, instead of hitting the snooze button and dragging themselves out of bed at the last moment possible every day, they'll set the alarm to go off an hour earlier and hit the gym before they go to work.

However, the majority of people can't sustain this 'full on' approach—if we could, we'd all be slim, toned and fit, right? Instead, what usually happens is this...

You set your alarm to go off early on the first morning, hit the gym, do your workout (whilst feeling slightly embarrassed because you're so out of shape in comparison to all the 'hard bodies' who look like they must live in there to be in the condition they're in!). However, you carry on, trying not to draw undue attention to yourself, finish your workout and head off to work feeling reasonably virtuous—after all, you got up early and worked out!

Next morning, it feels a little harder to get up when the alarm goes off and when you get out of bed, your muscles are sore and aching from the day before. You remember how embarrassed you felt about being out of shape. You remember that your stinky workout gear is still unwashed in the bottom of your gym bag and so you decide to give the gym a miss for that day. After all,

 The word 'Kaizen' means small, incremental steps of continuous improvement, . . .

you went yesterday and you'll definitely go tomorrow...

The morning after, however, you discover that your aches and pains are even worse (have you noticed how these things always feel worse on the second day?). So you decide you'll 'rest' for another day but you'll definitely get back to it tomorrow... And, of course, you never do.

And what about how, after sticking to your diet all day, you end up succumbing to a tasty, mid-afternoon treat and, then suddenly, you're wolfing down everything in sight, thinking that, since you've already broken your diet for today, you might as well stuff yourself stupid and start again with the diet tomorrow?

With that in mind, rather than going flat out in an 'all or nothing' approach to making changes in your life, can I suggest that you adopt a 'Kaizen' approach instead?

The word 'Kaizen' means small, incremental steps of continuous improvement, and it's generally applied to business processes—in fact I first learned about it years ago when I was studying education management. However I've since discovered that the concept of Kaizen can be applied to almost anything:

improving a relationship, clearing the house of clutter, building a home-based business, any task you've been procrastinating over – in fact, anything that could stand a little improvement.

Let's apply it to the area of health and wellness as an example.

Let's start off by making a list of all the things you know you SHOULD do (but, like most of us, probably don't) – you know the ones I mean, things like:

+ eating your five portions of fruit and vegetables every day
+ flossing your teeth
+ exercising for at least 30 minutes every day
+ cutting out sugar and sugar-laden drinks from your diet
+ drinking more water

Now, by asking you to make this list, I'm not trying to make you feel bad about all the things that you 'should' be doing or providing you with a stick to beat your guilty self with. The idea behind making a list is:

a) To give you a choice of things that you COULD do. The more choice you have, the easier it will be to make the right choice for you and, if it's the right choice, it'll be easier to sustain it and even build on it

b) To help you decide what would be the most beneficial area to start taking baby steps in. What will give you the most 'bang for your buck'?

c) To provide you with an ongoing list of things to do that you can come back to, again and again when you're ready to incorporate a new baby step into your life.

Then...

1. Choose one of your list items. Maybe it'll be the one that you think will have the biggest effect on your health and well-being. Or is there one that you feel particularly drawn to? Is there one that your intuition is telling you to do? Is there one that you're partially doing already and it would be easy to step up your efforts (for example, if you already eat 2 or 3 portions of fruit and vegetables every day, you might find it easy to add another portion or two).

2. Make a start today. Let's take our fruit and vegetables example again – your aim isn't to eat 5 portions of fruit and vegetables this very day. Because, if you currently eat NO f and v on a daily basis, then going from 0 to 5 in the course of a day ISN'T A BABY STEP—it's more like a giant leap! (And it'll be much harder to sustain, day after day.) A baby step would be something along the lines of—eat one extra piece of fruit today or eat the salad that comes with your burger instead of leaving it on your plate.

If you're not used to drinking water, a baby step would be drinking one glass or bottle of water over the course of the day or maybe substituting a glass of water for one of your usual soft drinks.

3. Once you've taken your baby step and your piece of fruit has been eaten or your glass of water drunk, pat yourself on the back. You did a good thing. You can feel virtuous for the rest of the day. Now all you need to do is rinse and repeat... Tomorrow, have another piece of fruit—maybe you could try a fruit that you've never tried before—you never know, you might find something delicious that will become a new favourite and make it easier for you to eat fruit more regularly. Or you could experiment with drinking water at various temperatures to find the most 'comfortable' temp for you. (That's not as daft as it sounds unless it's a very hot day. I don't like drinking very cold water. And in winter, I'm only likely to drink water if it's been allowed to 'warm up' to room temperature.)

The idea is to make each baby step a no-brainer. Something that you absolutely CAN do without having to battle against your resistance. Only YOU can decide on the size of your baby step. It has to be something that feels acceptable to you, something that you will be able to do easily and effortlessly. So you might need to experiment a little bit with the size of your baby steps. You may need to cut them in half or you may need to double them.

Give it a go. You don't need to use our health and wellness example. Choose another area of your life that could stand some improvement. Then just take that first step...

Ann Harrison (contemporaryretirement.typepad.com) is a Retirement Options™ trained retirement coach and Too Young To Retire™ facilitator. She is also a writer, blogger and creator of information products; she retired from her job in education management at the ripe old age of forty-three. She is the author of ebooks, "The Retirement Detox Programme: 40 days to get your retirement back on track" and 'Thought Provokers: Questions you need to ask yourself BEFORE you retire".

Making a Difference

"If your actions inspire others to dream more, learn more, do more and become more, you are a leader." - John Quincy Adams

Bertha Benz's Wild Ride

By DEBRA EVE (Los Angeles, California) 08 August 2012

Bertha Benz (1849-1944) had been married eighteen years when she took her husband's car for a spin—without his permission.

She was 39 years old and had just learned to drive. She planned to visit her mom, but needed help in case the car broke down, so she enlisted her teenage sons.

One morning before dawn, they rolled down the driveway so Mr. Benz wouldn't hear them, and off they went to Pforzheim, sixty miles away.

The year was 1888. There were no roads.

What was Bertha thinking as she sat behind the steering column en route to the Black Forest? Would her husband be mad, glad, insanely worried? That car was his baby.

Truly. It was the first one ever invented.

Others had attached an internal combustion engine to a horse carriage, but Carl Benz made the first vehicle designed for an engine. Bertha borrowed his third prototype, but he couldn't find buyers for it. The thing was just too scary. So he kept futzing and futzing.

No Roads. No Gas Stations. No Mechanics.

Bertha became exasperated with her genius husband and hatched her plan to visit mom, proving herself to be a brilliant marketing director for the fledgling Benz motorcar company.

She took to the road when there were no roads.

In Wiesloch, she stopped at a pharmacy to refuel, since gasoline was sold as cleaning fluid then.

In Bruchsal, she found a blacksmith to repair the snapped

drive chain.

In Bauschlott, she had a cobbler replace the leather on a brake shoe. While he was working, she telegrammed her now-frantic husband to let him know she and the baby were fine.

Somewhere along the route, she used her hatpin to clear a clogged fuel line and insulated a short-circuited wire with material from her garter.

At another point, her boys and a few local farmers pushed the car up a hill, since its 2.5 horsepower engine couldn't make it.

She arrived in Pforheim that same day after dusk (thank goodness, since it looks like the first Benz didn't have headlights) and informed her husband of their success.

The telegram probably read: "ARRIVED SAFE. MOTHER SENDS LOVE. ADD'L GEAR WOULD BE GOOD."

She became an immediate sensation. People lined the road on her return trip, some fascinated, others frightened by the hissing and spitting horseless carriage. But the automobile had proved its safety and utility.

Bertha's Legacy: One Billion Drivers

Germany holds a festival every two years to celebrate Bertha's historic journey. Since 2008, you can drive the Bertha Benz Memorial Route from Mannheim to Pforzheim via Heidelberg. It runs through the beautiful Baden wine region and signposts the milestones of Bertha's trip.

From age 22, when she invested her dowry in her husband's company, through age 39, when she pioneered the road trip, until her death at 95, Bertha Benz's daring helped birth an invention that changed our world (for better and worse).

Debra Eve (laterbloomer.com) is a proud late bloomer and possessor of many passions. At 36, she became an archaeologist. At 42, a martial arts instructor. At 46, she married the love of her life! Now she writes about fellow late bloomers while plotting her next grand adventure.

Chief Clarence Louie: Nation Builder

By CONNIE DENESIUK (Summerland, British Columbia) 03 May 2011

What a difference leadership can make.

In December 1984, the Osoyoos Indian Band was in financial trouble. Clarence Louie had just been elected as the band chief. He was just twenty-four years old. He had little experience to draw on but he was highly motivated. And, he had a hard work ethic. Four years later, he transformed the organization creating a multi-faceted corporation, which led his community on the path to self sufficiency. Today, the band owns nine businesses—a golf course, a cultural centre, a gas station and store, a construction company, a cement plant, a winery, RV park and campground and Spirit Ridge Vineyard Resort and Spa.

Recently, Chief Louie spoke to a group of Summerland citizens who were looking for insights into building a prosperous community. Those attending the Summerland Outlook conference certainly didn't come away disappointed.

"If every objection must be overcome," warned Chief Louie, "nothing will get done." Then he added, "Remember, it's the economic horse that pulls the social cart."

That mantra seems to sum up Chief Louie's economic development philosophy. Currently, the Osoyoos Band has 460 members, and every band member who wants a job has one. Hundreds of non-band members are also employed. With a view to the future, Chief Louie says "I make decisions based on what's good for the little ones."

Clarence Louie has been asked to speak throughout North America on the topic of economic development but he does a lot more than talk! Even though he is elected by members of the

Osoyoos Indian band, Chief Louie refuses to call himself a politician.

"I am not a politician," he said. "I am a worker. The difference between a politician and a leader is that politicians make promises about what they will do, while a leader tells people what they must do for themselves."

I asked Chief Louie what advice he would give to government regarding the aboriginal community. No surprise, but he was very clear in his response.

"Let us make decisions for ourselves," he stated. "We need autonomy."

When asked what advice he would give to young people, he said "You can only go as high as your work ethic will take you. Most successful people work 50 to 60 hours per week, so love your job or you will get bored easily."

As for the future, Chief Louie replied, "Opportunity comes from hard work and risk."

Truth be known, opportunity also comes from leaders like Chief Louie. No wonder the Globe and Mail selected Clarence Louie as one of the top ten nation builders of the past decade.

Connie Denesiuk *has a long history of community involvement in the Okanagan region of British Columbia. She brings a blend of common sense and optimism to her work. In addition to serving as a long time school trustee and as President of BC School Trustees Association, Connie and her husband Bob have been partners in their construction business for more than thirty years.*

Have You Had Your Hug Today?

By Melinda Schmitt (Raleigh, North Carolina) 31 May 2011

"An angel must have sent you to me," said the gas station attendant who just lost her mother the week before. "Thank you so much for that loving hug."

That is how I started the post I wrote for A Hopeful Sign only 50 days into a 365 day journey to spread joy and love through hugs. After all, love is what gives me hope.

My idea started out simply enough. I used to be a hugger as a child and I would hug anyone I came into contact with. A behavior I learned from my parents. Over the years, concerns over what other people would think or how they would react replaced my natural desire to hug. In the last few years, I watched others as they hugged. What I saw was rather eye opening. Those who seemed so happy and receptive to physical contact were often the ones to shrink from the hug, or release from the hug quickly. Those who were more reserved or closed off to contact seemed to appreciate this gesture much more. They would sink into the hug and hold on with such a look of gratitude on their faces, as if there was nowhere else they would rather be than in that moment.

Finally one day, lost in my own thoughts, it hit me. I needed to be hugging again and not just with my family. I needed to share this abundance of love that I possess with others. Less than one week later and with the advice and encouragement of my husband, my blog "My Year of Hugs" was created.

In less than five days, I received my first message about how my journey was impacting others. I met a very shy, reserved neighbor during our girls' night out. I thought my hug had made her uncomfortable and she wouldn't want anything more to do with me. Instead, I received this message from her friend:

"She had so much fun and talked more than she normally

does. She even commented on how much she liked you. I think your hug brought some walls down."

With this feedback I knew I was onto something. After that, I began receiving numerous other messages letting me know the impact I was having with them. And, they are not all coming from the people that I am actually hugging. Mostly they're from people who are reading about my hugs in the blog. I knew that I could create love around me by hugging, but I would only be able to reach a limited number of people. My hope was that people would receive the same feelings of love and joy by simply reading about them. It appears I was right. I have faithful followers that read my blog at night to end their days with joy and inspiration. I have received messages that have brought tears to my eyes and others that make my heart overflow with love.

To my amazement I have found significant changes in my own life. Every day I seem to be happier than the last. Every day I wake to the excitement that I can make a difference in someone's life. Every day I am more courageous and confident. I began this journey in hopes that I would bring some joy and love to others. Little did I know the impact it would have on me.

A few months after the year ended my story spread across the globe. This simple idea of hugging struck a chord in people throughout the world with its universally understood message of love. I was contacted by friends from Brazil, Vietnam, Israel, India, and more. What makes me hopeful? Realizing that love may in fact be all we need.

Melinda Schmitt (myyearofhugs.com) is a dedicated mother with two beautiful young boys and the creator of her blog "my year of hugs". Melinda's goal is to spread joy and happiness through the power of a hug–one day and one person at a time.

Meet George the Cabbie

By SHARON REED (Davidson, North Carolina) 06 September 2011

Every now and then, a stranger crosses our path, sometimes just for a mere moment, and we catch a glimpse of greatness. We catch a glimpse of what it means to serve others with a glad heart, a lively spirit, and personal integrity. We catch someone 'getting it right' and we want to share their story. So it is with George the cabbie.

I met George last weekend in Orlando, while standing in line outside my hotel, waiting to catch the bus that ran between the hotel and convention center. Buses ran every thirty minutes, and all of us standing in line were anxious to arrive in time to hear the morning keynote speaker.

The bus came, picked up five people, then announced it was full, pulling away and leaving the rest of us waiting in earnest for another bus. Impatiently, I turned to my new friend Lorin and asked if she wanted to grab a taxi instead. She agreed and within seconds, we were joined by Peter from Japan and Jan from Belgium.

Quickly we piled into the nearby cab, my leg still hanging slightly out the door on the verge of doing a slight split, when the driver George started to pull away. We were nonetheless greeted with a smile when George jokingly assured me he had insurance, just in case I needed it. We were off, and in the span of a less-than-five-minute drive, we had all managed to introduce ourselves and pass out cards, including George. Without being pushy, George also managed to pass around a spiral notebook in which he asked us to write our names, numbers, and departure flights.

At this point, I had been collecting cabbie cards throughout the previous few days, including one from Samuel, who shared stories of his hurricane-wrecked homeland of Haiti, various relief efforts, and his perception of the Americans who have extended a hand to help rebuild.

"Who" Samuel had asked, "comes and serves others so selflessly, and with such love and generosity? People don't do that much anymore, but your people do."

I liked Samuel, and though George was courteous and entertaining, I wasn't ready to commit my transportation needs to him. Instead, I politely filled in my name and number, telling George that while I was leaving the next day, I wasn't prepared to make firm plans.

Departure day:

Eating an early breakfast with my girlfriend, I remembered that I had not yet made taxi arrangements, though I was scheduled to fly out just before noon. I quickly retrieved Samuel's card and dialed his number, to no avail.

Hmmm. What other cards had I saved? Before I could even look for another number, my phone rang.

It was George. "Good morning, Ms. Reed. I remembered you were flying home today and wondered if you have already made

 Sometimes, amazing things can happen when you take a leap of faith. Even on the little things.

transportation arrangements, and if not, if I could be of service to you?"

"Absolutely," I exclaimed, and proceeded to give him instructions for picking me up outside of the convention center at 9:45 a.m. He reconfirmed the time and promised to call me at 9:40 a.m. to let me know he was five minutes out.

9:40 a.m.

My phone rings, though I missed the call because I still had my phone on silent. I listen to the message. It's George. "Hi, Ms. Reed. It's George. I apologize, but I am running five minutes late. I realize that there is a line of cabs outside of the convention center, but I'm asking if you will please wait for me. I have confirmed with the airport that the lines are short and the traffic is light. I promise you will get there in plenty of time."

I called him back and agreed to wait for him. He recommended that I wait inside where it was cool, and promised to call when he was within one minute of arriving. And so he did.

He told me on the way to the airport that most people would not have waited for him, and he greatly appreciated my willingness to do so. I admit that I took a chance, and for a brief moment while I was waiting for him to arrive, I wondered to myself: should I trust his word? If I'm wrong, I will miss my flight and it will cost me hundreds of dollars and a great deal of wasted time. But if he's being honest, then I want to deliver on my end of the deal. I won't sell him out to someone who hasn't earned the business. Sometimes, amazing things can happen when you take a leap of faith. Even on the little things. Like a cab ride to the airport. As he pulled up to the airport, he reminded me to stay safe, gave me a big hug and bid me a pleasant farewell.

End of the story? Not quite...

True to his word, the lines were short and I had plenty of time before my flight took off. Feet sore from three days of walking endlessly around in high heels, I got to my gate, dropped my bags, took off my shoes, and breathed a sigh of exhaustion. Just then, my phone buzzed, indicating a text had arrived. From George. "Hi! This is George. I just wanted to wish you a safe trip home."

A chance encounter. A random cab. An unknown driver. Four initial passengers. At least two repeat passengers (and loyal passengers for life). One referral passenger. As I picked up the last text from George, I smiled deeply and thought to myself, "George gets it."

Life is so much more than just an exchange of goods and services. At its heart, life is about people. It's about connections. It's about service. It's about living, leading and serving from the heart.

Sharon Reed (heartpath.wordpress.com) is a global and civic-minded strategist who writes and speaks on living and leading a heart-aligned life. She is passionate about building bridges of understanding and empowering others to make a positive difference in the world – through communication, connection, education and engagement. Sharon is also the founder and chief editor of the Global Girls Project, a collaborative writing project dedicated to empowering women and girls around the world through stories of heart-aligned leadership (www.globalgirlsproject.org). Sharon lives in Davidson, NC with her two children, Michael and Allison.

Mrs. Hand: The Teacher Who Handed Us a Whole New World

By HEATHER ONDERICK (Barcelona, Spain) 27 July 2011

I remember us curled up on the carpet with heads perched on our hands, toes pointed up in the air making lofty circles while Mrs. Hand read us the old novel, *My Side of the Mountain.* She brought out a similar survival kit to Sam Gribley's and over recesses and book talks, we all began to feel as if we were Sam's side-kick, conquering the great outdoors with him, reenacting scenes and collecting food and firewood for our next adventure.

It was nearly halfway through the school year and all of us were a little skeptical about the "new" teacher. Mrs. Hand had just returned from medical leave and we only knew her by reputation.

And Mrs. Hand was one of those teachers who had a reputation. Her students loved or hated her. There were stories: ones about Mrs. Hand putting kids in boxes for punishment and making you do 100 pages of times tables per night. To this day I have no idea where children get these stories, even the likes of Mrs. Trunchbull and Miss Viola Swamp are not as bad as some of the stories we concoct as children.

Mrs. Hand taught me during 4th grade at Centennial Road Elementary in Scarborough, Ontario, a suburb of Toronto. She was a diamond in a field of gems. When I look back at my elementary experiences, I remember Mrs. Hand. I remember 4th grade and I remember exactly how we learned. The particular unit that I remember most is the one I have also had the privilege to teach. We were studying the culture and geography of Canada, with required focus on the province of residence.

Over weeks, we made bedazzled 3-D topographical maps of Ontario which challenged us to become architects, landscape designers and artists simultaneously. And it only got better: the culture portion of that unit contributed to me becoming the international person I am today. You see, Mrs. Hand wanted her classmates to see a whole new world outside of the one we regularly learned about in the classroom. So, we explored in a "Magic School Bus" sort of way. We started down in Chinatown, sampling dried ginseng chips and candied ginger in the Asian market. Following another culinary scent, we ended up singing Christmas carols with a Chinese Santa while warming our fingers on the roasted chestnuts crumbling in our hands from the food stand. The next day was even better. In Cabbagetown, with sugared orange in our hands, we learned about the fate of Irish potato farmers who had started farming cabbage to survive the cold winters and feed their families. We moved on to our last stop, Kensington market, where we partook in Jewish dancing, learned the history of housing projects and immigrants from around the world who now resided in the community. Mrs. Hand introduced us to history through personal stories, food, maps and photography; so much more

 In Russia, although I was a mere 14 years old, I longed to listen to the stories of the children at the orphanage.

than what a textbook provides.

It wasn't until five years later when I was inspired to do an AFS cultural exchange that I realized how much Mrs. Hand had changed my life. In Russia, although I was a mere 14 years old, I longed to listen to the stories of the children at the orphanage. I looked at their photos and their trinkets and pieced them together with questions to try to complete the puzzles of these orphans' lives. When asked to participate in an all-city dance competition in Russia, my friends and I didn't hesitate. "This is like going to the park on the weekend for them," I said to my friend Mary about the contest with 1000 children participants. When it was finished I said, "I'm pretty sure this is better."

So, Mrs. Hand, here I am nearly 22 years later and the world is truly at my hands. I am 30 years old and have travelled to more than 30 different countries. I am teaching 5th grade in Barcelona, Spain at the American School of Barcelona and I try to inspire my students' curiosity in the world just like you did for me.

You showed me truly how important understanding different people and different places are, and the best part is you made it immensely fun.

The world needs more teachers like you.

Heather Onderick is an educator and world traveler who has visited over 30 different countries. She is an avid runner, loves art, photography, yoga and Thai food. Heather has a Bachelors degree in Fine Arts from Hamilton College in Upstate New York and a Master's in Education from Jones International University, based out of Colorado. She also writes her own blog inspired by her travels, teaching and cooking adventures, called Teach, Cook, Explore.

Why Did I Become an Educator?

By CARRIE ELLEN BRUMMER (Dubai, UAE) 19 June 2011

Over my seven year career as an art teacher I have been asked a few times: Why did you become a teacher? Some people ask me out of curiosity while others look at me like I'm a Petri dish growing exotic fungi, or worse, an infectious disease.

There are many reasons for having different approaches to this question. For instance, when I tell my sister Anne I love teenagers, she gives me this funny look. She once teased, "Wait until you have your own." I think many people freeze in horror at the notion of holding 20-something 16 year olds captive for an hour or more. And perhaps to some that may be torture (I'm sure the students sometimes feel that way!). For me, I love the questioning, the slight (or not so slight) desire to rebel, and I love watching young people self-discover. Teenagers make me laugh and smile nearly every day.

Another reason some may ask is because of the nature of the profession (think income). Several people have confided in me they would go into teaching if it paid more. So, why would I do it, even if the pay can be questionable?

I teach because I want to serve others. I am fulfilled when I see a student push outside his or her comfort zone and risk sharing their opinion or something personal. It is especially rewarding when I receive a note like this:

Hi Ms. Brummer! I just wanted to show you a video that a friend sent me about this artists' journey, it's so good! Haha, but I won't spoil it for you. Thank you for such a wonderful year and for helping me throughout my journey as an artist. It's a good feeling to be able to depend on the kind of direction you offer, so thank you again, and I look forward to spending another with you! (:

I teach because I want to make a difference in the lives of others. I worked at a charter public school in the USA prior to my job in Dubai. I loved my school but there were some challenging students who needed a lot of support. There were days I dreaded going to work because I just wasn't ready to face their energy! Several years ago I received this note from one of those students:

I wanted to thank you for everything Ms. Brummer. I honestly don't think that there is any other teacher that I've had that has changed my life more so than I thought. In other words you helped me go in a direction I don't think I would've pursued because of how it is looked at by the "older" generation. I'm also writing this to you because in my human communications class we have to give a speech about someone who inspired us in our lives and I chose you because of how you pushed me without really using force but by encouragement and advice. So I thank you Ms. Brummer for everything and I still think that Jean-Michel Basquiat is the best artist of his time despite what others would say. Oh and the title of my speech is, "Brandon, what are you doing?"

I teach because it matters. While I'm not always so lucky to receive notes like the ones above, I've seen the impact of a lifelong educator. My uncle, William Brummer, was an educator who had no idea how many lives he had touched and was actively wondering about his worth as a teacher when he died. At his funeral, literally hundreds of students left notes, sent flowers, or were physically present for the ceremony. Our profession, his role as an educator, mattered.

Why did I become an educator? Because I want to positively impact the lives of others.

I know countless people who have had their lives touched by an educator. For me it was Mr. Fuller (Middle School English at Avon Middle School…I have tried to find you! Thank you, wherever you are). If you want to positively impact the life of someone, send that note of appreciation you've always thought about writing but never did. As an educator I can promise you: it means more than you know.

Carrie Ellen Brummer (artistthink.com) is an artist, a teacher, and a dreamer. She has been teaching Visual Arts for 8 years to students who have enriched her life! Carrie is also a practicing artist who has had art exhibits in both the United States and Dubai.

Me to We: Student Leadership in Action

By PAIGE SKOFTEBY (Salmon Arm, British Columbia) 02 May 2011

I am a member of the School District 83 student leadership team working with Free the Children. Free the Children is an organization helping less fortunate children and creating awareness for more fortunate students. Free the Children's mission is to "empower youth everywhere to make a difference through leadership training at home and community development projects abroad."

We are excited to say that through our District wide program, "Toonie Tuesday" we have raised approximately $30,000.00. Because we are a "for the children, by the children" charitable organization the student committee chose to work with Free the Children and support both local and global projects. We have fully adopted a village in Sierra Leone, an extremely poor county in Africa. We met our goal and raised enough funds to build a school and supply water. This year our committee has decided to put our funds raised toward adopting a village in Kenya.

Supporting local organizations is also very important. To get funds to support local projects, schools must submit requests to the District Student leadership interview committee. With the help of our leadership teacher, Mrs. Ellis, my school gave back and created awareness by making sandwiches for our local food bank, having a pancake breakfast for donation and participating in "one night out" which created awareness about homelessness. Our local focus this year as a district is to provide leadership retreats through Free the Children's sacred circle program for our Aboriginal students. We hope to have Aboriginal student

 You have no idea what freedom is until you've lost it or it has been taken from you

representation on our district committee next year. 700 students and adults from our district had the privilege to attend "We Day" sponsored by Free the Children in Vancouver over the past two years. This was the most moving experience EVER. Before I had ever been to "We Day" I didn't realize how bad poverty and child labor was because it wasn't around me; Marc and Craig Kielburger really opened my eyes and showed me how lucky we are and we don't even know it. These brothers formed Free the Children at a very young age and have grown it into a worldwide network to help this generation become more compassionate.

I enjoy being involved with the District Student Leadership-Me to We team to help others around the world and to help people in our community become more aware. My most memorable moment was when Craig Kielburger said, *You have no idea what freedom is until you've lost it or it has been taken from you.*

Paige Skofteby is a Grade 8 student enrolled at Carlin Elementary Middle School in the North Okanagan-Shuswap School District in British Columbia.

Students "Make Art for Change"

By JENNIFER CACACI (Kamloops, British Columbia) 31 January 2012

High School Art Students at South Kamloops Secondary really put their hearts into their recent class project. Starting with the belief: "Art changes people. People change the world," a dedicated group of girls set their sights on women in poverty. After thoughtful research and dynamic class discussions, these junior art students believed they could create artworks to reflect, not just the problems girls and women face, but their belief in the strength of women and how they can be the catalysts of change.

Students were encouraged to look at different regions around the world and research some of the specific hardships girls and women endure. Next, students looked at the positive actions taken by humanitarian groups/organizations, empowering women through education and financial aid. The students quickly recognized that a lot of people are actively involved; empowering, supporting and inspiring women!

The next step was image development and the question of how to arrange images and colours to create a compelling message; how to reveal hardships and yet suggest hope. In the end, this project engaged the students to think creatively and to think with empathy. For the students, the more they believed in the message, the more they challenged themselves to improve their technical skills and understanding of the principles of art. They really believed in the images they created, and in the potential to communicate something bigger than themselves. For me, it was inspiring to see this; to listen to their dialogue and watch as they created twenty five, diverse and uniquely compelling artworks!

"134 million children between the ages of 7-18 have never been to school. Girls are more likely to go without schooling than boys. In the Middle East and North Africa, girls are much more likely than boys

to be denied access. My artwork represents girls who deserve a chance at education. I painted an open book with women holding hands in the background. Listed on the book is some of the countries in poverty. I believe if girls were given more of a chance to go to school they could help change the world and inspire more girls to get a good education." (Dakota, Grade 9)

"In my artwork, I chose to represent Somalia. I did this by incorporating tigers, an African border, and people wearing African war masks. I used water color and ink to mix together bright patterns. My painting is supposed to show how fiercely women can fight to break through poverty if they are given the chance. Every day, terrible things happen to over 1 000 women in Somalia. Only 24% of woman are literate and 1 in 10 woman risk dying during pregnancy. Many woman are forced into prostitution to help support their families, and 97% of female prostitutes start before the age of 14. Even though many women are never given a chance to be great, they still shine on the inside, and the hand of a man will never be able to force down that power." (Jaymee, Grade 10)

"If one woman can change her life and make a difference in the lives of others, imagine what 3.3 million strong and capable women can do.... My painting is meant to replicate this idea. The woman in my painting is strong and holding a tool of power- the hammer. With the hammer she strikes a glass ball. The ball is a symbol of poverty, and everything women must fight to be free and independent. The tip of the hammer is immersed in blue flames. These flames are a literal and figurative representation of the force women can make. Overall my painting is a demonstration of the impact women can make as individuals and as a group." (Morgan, Grade 10)

Ultimately, the students posted their images to our blog, Make Art For Change. They worked through the challenging process of titling and writing artist statements to support their artwork. Then, using Facebook and Twitter we tackled getting the message "out there". As a classroom teacher it is often my goal to get artwork viewed beyond the classroom walls, but getting it out to the world through the internet was really exciting!

Thank you to those who have viewed Make Art For Change and helped to share our message of hope.

Jennifer Cacaci, (makeartforchange.blogspot.com) teaches Art at South Kamloops Secondary in British Columbia.

Change the World in 3 Minutes

By GARY DOI (Penticton, British Columbia) 29 May 2011

Three minutes. 180 seconds. Not a lot of time.

Yet, three-minutes can be life altering, affecting your path and that of others. For example, a convincing three minute elevator speech could make the difference between getting and not getting that new job. Or, what about that person you've admired from afar? They say it only takes three minutes to create a lasting first impression. Or, consider a life-threatening house fire. Research shows you only have three minutes or less to get out alive. Hence, the three-minute drill.

What else are three-minutes good for? Award-winning media teacher Russ Stasiuk from Penticton Secondary School in the Okanagan Valley has a good use for three-minutes: "Create a three-minute video that changes the world in a hopeful way," he says to his senior students. "You can take a micro or macro approach. Go big or go small. It doesn't matter. The only rule is that it must be three minutes or less and include the words — A Hopeful Sign — in the title."

Then, as an afterthought, he adds, "Oh yes, the top three videos will be featured on a new magazine blog called A Hopeful Sign."

The change-the-world project creates a sharp focus for the students and they rise to the challenge:

Sarah Petreny (grade 10) and Jaime Naylor (grade 12) tackle the subject of friendship and its importance to their well-being. "Friends can be counted upon for fun, love, and support," says Sarah.

"That's right," adds her video partner Jaime Naylor. "We have so many negative things in our society today, and taking a moment to think of the positives — like friends — help us cherish them more."

Grade 11 student Layne Richardson travelled to Africa last

summer and captures that experience in his video. "In many places in Africa," says Layne, "orphanages are like Starbucks; there is one on every street. These children have gone through many things in their lives that nobody should have to go through, ever. Many people are doing what they can to help out."

Still, Layne is amazed how resilient the children are. "No matter how badly these kids have been abused, they always have a smile," he says. "They are extremely happy to have what they have, even though it is very minimal."

Grade 12 student Jordan Findlay approaches his video project from a historical perspective.

"I think that hope is something that has to be found within a person; inspiration to ignite this hope can spawn from many different angles," says Jordan. "I selected an approach which was broad and spanned different struggles, eras, and individuals. I tried to use an array of images to inspire the reader to think about hope and show how other people in history have influenced hopeful movements."

Jordan also comments about the negativity in the world and what the blog "A Hopeful Sign" was trying to do. "It's good to know that there is a magazine blog like that," he says. "It helps us celebrate our accomplishments and the power of human perseverance."

Changing the world may seem like an impossible mission to most adults but not to young people like Sarah, Jaime, Layne and Jordan. To them, the future is about opportunity, possibility and change. It is about engaging life with wholehearted authenticity, honesty and integrity. It is about hope and perseverance.

It is about changing the world in three minutes.

Gary Doi served as Superintendent of Schools for eighteen years in three school districts in British Columbia. Previous to that, he was a teacher, school administrator and university lecturer. He created the magazine blog, "A Hopeful Sign" (ahopefulsign.com), as he believes there is no greater force for creating change than hope.

Hope Heals at Ted E. Bear Hollow

By NANCY HEMESATH (Omaha, Nebraska) 01 July 2011

At Ted E. Bear Hollow, we have a saying that we are putting on T-shirts: "Hope Heals." It all started in 2001, when our co-founders, Joy and Marv Johnson, were asked to do something for the grieving children in our own community of Omaha, Nebraska. They had been making trips with Centering Corporation's (centering.org) grief support materials to Oklahoma City after the bombing, Columbine, Colorado, after the school shooting, and New York City after 9/11. They were the experts who helped these cities deal with the aftermath of tragedies, especially the grief residing in the hearts of children left behind.

Yet, in Omaha and the surrounding area, children and teens were also struggling with death due to cancer, heart disease, accidents, suicide and homicides. No community is immune from untimely deaths and few adults understand how to support their children through the grief, especially when they are grieving too. Families were asking for help beyond an occasional camp experience.

Joy Johnson saw that it was time to initiate a non-profit that would provide help for children, teens and families who were struggling with grief. Children's grief centers were popping up around the country as others saw the same need in their own cities. Portland, Oregon, was first in 1982 and others soon followed. People of courage around the country were seeing the need and stepping up.

Joy pulled together friends who knew and loved children and were willing to roll up their sleeves. Once the non-profit was established, the core group educated themselves about children's grief. Then they decorated the little building owned by the

Johnsons so that they were ready for groups to begin. The first support group was announced and the self-taught facilitators stood ready. Would anybody come? They opened the door at the assigned time and there was a line extending out to the street and down the sidewalk.

Since then thousands of grieving children have discovered they are not alone. Other kids their own age understand what they are going through. Their adult caregivers have discovered new life among supportive peers. Thousands of deceased loved ones have been memorialized in handmade picture frames, on pillow cases, decoupage boxes, and scrapbook pages – all because it is now okay for children to share their memories. Friendships have been forged as families adapt to the "new normal." Through this process hope is restored and "hope heals" broken hearts.

The power of this work cannot be overestimated. Families consistently report that they see positive changes in their children who come to Ted E. Bear Hollow programs. Without support in dealing with unresolved grief, youth are at high risk for illness, depression, and negative behaviors such as substance abuse, promiscuity, and illegal activity. Ted E. Bear Hollow diverts this negative energy into hopefulness. Imagine our job satisfaction as we watch the transformation time after time!

We are indebted to the founding board who took the risk of starting this venture on behalf of vulnerable children. The seed planted has grown and is now housed in a lovely facility provided by Children's Hospital & Medical Center. Ted E. Bear Hollow now has six staff members and hundreds of trained volunteers. We never charge families because no child should grieve alone.

Nancy Hemesath (tedebearhollow.org) served as Ted E. Bear Hollow's first executive director from 2005 to 2013. Nancy was instrumental in helping the agency to significantly increase its capacity to serve the community. She stepped down from leadership to work part-time in promoting the work of Ted E. Bear Hollow in communities surrounding Omaha. Nancy is originally from Iowa but has lived in Omaha for more than two decades. She received her Master's Degree from Boston College. Prior to joining TEBH, Nancy was the executive director of Habitat for Humanity of Omaha for seven years. She has also held various administrative positions at The College of St. Mary, including Director of Student Services. Nancy serves as board member for The National Alliance for Grieving Children. Nancy feels that supporting grieving children is her "best life's work."

Commemorating the 3/11 Tohoku Earthquake Disaster

By AIMEE LEDEWITZ WEINSTEIN (Tokyo, Japan) 05 March 2013

"After a major disaster, physical and emotional healing co-exist," explains Sophia Slater. "One can't exist without the other." To some adults, this might seem like common sense, but Sophia Slater is a sixteen-year-old junior at the American School in Japan (ASIJ) and experience has made her wise beyond her years. As the second anniversary of the March 11th Tohoku Earthquake approaches, she is focused more than ever on the community service initiative she founded, called Charmworks, that provides aid to people affected by the disaster.

During and after the earthquake, Sophia had her own problems. She was at school at the time, and on a good day with no traffic, ASIJ is almost an hour outside of the city of Tokyo, where she has lived all her life. Getting back home that day, with the snarled traffic and non-working infrastructure, took over eight hours. She had worries about her own family and their safety, as well as that of her friends. But within a short time, her mind turned to how she could help those who were truly suffering in the north of Japan, in the Tohoku region.

"Sometimes ways of giving are limited by who you are," Sophia explains with a practical bent. "I had to figure out the best way for me, a teenager, to make even a small difference."

Funakoshi – Before and After the Tsunami

Renowned for its slate and seaweed, the small fishing village of Funakoshi in the Tohoku region of Japan is still unrecognizable two years after the earthquake and subsequent tsunami. There had been 130 families living there but the entire town was obliterated. An NGO called "It's Not Just Mud" that did work in the region put Sophia in touch with the people who used to live in the town. Those people were coming into town daily, some of them traveling upwards of sixty minutes from their temporary housing, to work together to start rebuilding. First, they needed money. The men of the town started clearing out homes and salvaging roof tiles made from the precious slate. They then cut the slate into small, round pieces, and the women of the town starting painting them to sell as charms. These men and women now work six days a week making charms, and these days, can't fulfill all of the orders they get for the delightful slate charms. That's where Sophia comes in. Twice a month she organizes people in Tokyo to paint charms. The people of Funakoshi send her blank circles of slate and she sells the circles painted with designs made by people of all ages, of all backgrounds, just wanting to do something to help Tohoku. She then sends the money up to Funakoshi.

Prior to painting the charms together, Sophia explains, the people were working independently to earn money to rebuild the village. Once someone came up with the idea of making the

 "I had to figure out the best way for me, a teen-ager, to make even a small difference."

charms, the men and women who had previously had a community based on proximity, were able to re-form their community based on shared love of their town. That's where the emotional healing is coming into play, according to Sophia. Each of the people is safe and warm and they are re-starting their lives in various ways. But that doesn't make them miss the loved ones they lost any less. And it doesn't make them forget the bonds they once shared. Now they are able to tie together the physical work of earning money to try to buy the fishing boats, nets, and other equipment needed to re-start their industry with the emotional needs of healing their souls. The two types of healing co-exist.

Anyone who wants to buy a charm to support Funakoshi can do so by contacting Sophia via the Charmworks website, *www. charmworks.org*. They run between $7 and $12, and you can request certain designs or symbols be put on your charm.

Sophia is quick to say that she doesn't want credit for starting

Charmworks or making the charms. She wants all of the recognition to go to the men and women of Funakoshi, who are moving forward with rebuilding their lives. She is just a conduit to getting more charms made and sold for them. All of the money she earns from the charms goes directly back to the town of Funakoshi. She is quite an amazing young lady to have taken on this type of bi-monthly commitment to help this town, and she does it with the grace of a young woman who is on the brink of a bright future, one charm at a time.

Dr. Aimee Weinstein (TokyoWriter.com) is a writer and writing professor who has lived eight out of the last ten years in Tokyo, Japan. She received her doctorate from the Department of Higher Education at George Mason University and has held positions at Temple University Japan, The George Washington University, and George Mason University. She has taught a variety of writing courses, from freshman composition to advanced expository writing. Her work has been published in Kaleidescope, Tokyo Weekender, inTouch, and Asian Jewish Life. She also maintains a regular blog where she fondly observes Tokyo life through the eyes of an American expat and writes about writing. Aimee currently resides in Tokyo with her supportive husband and two beautiful children, where she continues to write and help others in their writing.

LWB in Guatemala

By SAMHITA GUPTA (Toronto, Ontario) 20 May 2011

"We can't repay you for the work you've done here, but we hope that the love of reading that this library will foster among the children is repayment."

Through these memorable words Jorge Chojolan, founder and principal of the Miguel Asturias Academy in Quetzaltenango (Xela), Guatemala, expressed his gratitude to us, twenty-seven students from Librarians Without Borders (LWB) chapters in University of Toronto, McGill, Dalhousie and Western. It was the evening of Friday,

April 29th, our last day in Xela, and we had just finished presenting to Jorge the work that we had done for the school's library over the course of that week.

Jorge had hit the nail on the head with his words. To ignite the love of reading, learning and knowledge in young minds was a goal that inspired each one of us sitting there on the library carpet listening to Jorge, and that bound us as a team. And the acute importance of this goal — particularly in the political and social context of Guatemala — was reiterated in our hearts on our first day at the school when, over the sounds of children at recess, Jorge talked to us about education in Guatemala and the school's mission and philosophy.

It quickly became clear to us that our work at the library was part of a much larger project that we shared with the Asturias Academy. We realized that the collection that we had contributed — over 350 books — had to be supplemented with a structure that would enable a culture of reading and learning. In Guatemala the quality of and access to education is poor, and a culture of learning and valuing education is absent due to a confluence of factors: a historical lack of governmental support for education, poverty, systemic marginalization of indigenous communities, and gender inequality that has been entrenched in social norms. Asturias is a non-profit, non-governmental institution that is committed to counter this state of affairs by providing students who would not otherwise afford an education with free or partially funded education that has a special focus on teaching students to be critically aware and reflective of their social reality.

So, after some intense brainstorming on the first day, the twenty-seven of us split up into sub-groups and not only did we completely catalogue their library, we also helped Steve, the librarian, implement new measures to promote student engagement with the library and its resources. A K'iche' (the prevalent Mayan indigenous language in the Xela region) audiobook project was introduced with the goal of preserving and promoting oral indigenous culture. Since the school plans to eventually open up the library to the community at large, some of us worked on a user-needs assessment project focussing on identifying issues with regard to the user community that would inform future collection development.

Jorge was right. The outcome towards which we worked will

indeed be reward for our efforts. But equally rewarding was the very experience of living in Xela and working with the Asturias community, using our skills to play a part in the school's mission, and broadening our perspectives.

Samhita Gupta *graduated with a Masters in Library and Information Studies from the University of Toronto in 2012. She is deeply interested in the role libraries play in promoting literacy and lifelong learning. For more information about LWB (Librarians Without Borders) check out the website lwb-online.org*

The Price of Hope

By ZEE GORMAN (San Francisco, California), 03 September 2011

In May 2011, The International Federation for Human Rights (FIDH) issued a report on human rights abuses during the Egyptian Revolution. It found that between January and February of 2011, 846 people died, 6,467 were injured and an unidentifiable number of people were arbitrarily arrested and tortured. The title of the report was "The Price of Hope".

Roughly 20 years ago in China, a similar event happened.

Observing the peaceful protests from his office, a foreigner predicted government crackdown. This foreigner was Mr. Nakamura, my boss in a Chinese-Japanese joint venture in Shenzhen, China, where I served as his secretary.

I remember those days vividly.

It was the late 1980's. China's economic reforms brought outcries for more comprehensive reforms. The notion was widespread – from university students to even some government officials. And yet it was suppressed. In April 1989, upon the death of one such government official who was an advocate of rapid reforms, the students took to Tiananmen Square to protest. Among their demands: freedom of speech and political reforms.

The government continued to pay only lip service which angered the students. In May the Tiananmen Square protesters went on hunger strike. All around China hundreds of thousands rose up to their support.

Every day after work, I rushed to the campus of Shenzhen University where I had worked as a language instructor. I met with other faculty members and students and we talked about how to support the student movement. Universities in all major cities were mobilized and student representatives were sent to Beijing. The President of Shenzhen University took the lead of the Beijing delegation. A massive demonstration in the city of Shenzhen was planned.

The day before the demonstration, I went to Mr. Nakamura to ask for leave.

"Mr. Nakamura, you know what's going on in China right now, right?"

"Of course," he said.

"May I have a few days off to participate? We have a demonstration tomorrow."

"No," he simply said.

"What? Why?" I hardly ever asked for time off. I couldn't believe that for something so important, he would deny my request.

"Because you've told me why you need the days off, I can't approve your days off." His reasoning was beyond the comprehension of this hot-headed twenty-something-year-old. I was speechless. Having been his secretary for two years, I had gained his trust and built a great rapport with him. I had never seen him so cold and unsupportive of me.

I followed him around and continued to plead for my case. "Please Mr. Nakamura, don't you think that freedom of speech and democracies are important causes?"

"It's none of my business. This is your country and I have no opinion one way or another."

"Then why do you care what I do? Why can't I go?"

"I don't care!" He raised his voice. Then he lowered it. "I care about this company. If your government cracks down, I don't want this company to have anything to do with it. I don't want to be even near it." I knew how hard he had worked to make the company successful. I didn't see the risk.

I shook my head. "They won't crack down on this one. This is too big. And what we ask for is reasonable!"

He looked me in the eye. "I studied your history. You don't understand. . . ." The way he looked at me momentarily stunned me. He was dead serious. "Show up to work tomorrow or you're fired," was his final words.

That put me in a quandary. I loved my job. It was my first corporate job. More importantly, I was the first in my family to experience what it was like to work in a non-socialist environment. I treasured the sense of accomplishment it afforded me.

I showed up for work the next day, but I was angry at Mr. Nakamura.

Then the following day, I called in sick.

"What's wrong with you?" he asked me over the phone.

"I'm pregnant!" I shouted. *You want me to lie. You get a big fat lie.*

There was silence on the other end. Finally he said, "I heard abortion is pretty painful. Take care and I'll see you in two weeks."

I took a train to Guangzhou where massive protests went on for days. I stayed with my parents there. Towards the beginning of June, the tone on all television channels subtly changed.

I was sitting in my parents' living room and watching the news on the television. There were reports about riots. Armed forces were dispatched to Beijing to maintain order. Then there was a report about mobs killing the soldiers of the People's Liberation Army (PLA) and burning them alive. There were images of a burned soldier's body hanging from a bridge. They were played again and again.

I knew too well what this all meant: The government had taken control of the media. I rushed back to Shenzhen. I needed to be with my friends.

The next day, martial law was declared and tanks rolled into Tiananmen square. Word spread like wild fire that soldiers had opened fire and many protesters had died. We knew what was ahead and we decided that we would not go quietly into the night. That evening we took to the campus, tore up as many white shirts and bed sheets as we could find and tied them on trees. We asked onlookers to help and they took off their shirts . . . We wanted the whole campus covered by these white ribbons for people to see when they woke up the next day. We worked until dawn. Then the following day, the white ribbons spread. People spotted them in other locations of the city.

. . .

In mid-June I returned to work. I walked into Mr. Nakamura's office and he gestured for me to sit down. He did not look up from his desk. After a long moment of silence, he said, "I'm sorry."

I wanted to cry. I felt like a fool because he was right. I felt ashamed at what my government did. And above all I felt angry. I felt angry because my hope was crushed into a thousand pieces.

"I'll get back to work." I stood up.

By then all activities associated with the "June Fourth Incident" were declared anti-government. A comprehensive lock down and investigation ensued. The President of Shenzhen University was arrested, together with several of his associates. Many were black-listed. The cleansing for sympathizers reached every corner. On official record, I was not a member of the faculty and I was on sick leave.

What was the price of hope? For me, it was disappointment and embarrassment; for many others, it was their freedom and even their lives.

Should we abandon hope?

To answer that let me quote Ilio Durandis of Haitian Times:

"Let us never live without hope, for the moment we stop hoping is the time we stop breathing. As long as we are alive, we shall survive, and survival is founded on the premise of hope. Together, let us hope for a better tomorrow. Let's join hands in unison, and chant the song of hope, even if it would cost us our lives, we shall never cease to hope."

Zee Gorman (zeegorman.blogspot.ca) *born in South China during the Cultural Revolution (both her parents were exiled to the countryside for being 'intellectuals'), was raised within layers of political and cultural confines. Yet her love for literature gave wings to a life that would be completely different from that of her parents. She has written short stories, poems, and essays, and is mildly published in China. Her quest and thirst for more understanding of the Western cultures eventually led to her migration to the United States where she completed two Master's Degrees at Northern Arizona University. Today, Zee Gorman lives in Northern California with her husband and her daughter. By night she is a writer, an artist, a crafter… whatever she imagines herself to be and by day she has a career in IT management.*

Made in the USA
Charleston, SC
04 November 2013